# CAMINO

Reimagining the Path

*Travelista Liz*

CAMINO: Reimagining the Path

Copyright © 2019 Liz Harvey

Published by: Desert Peaks LLC

Editor: Mary L. Holden

Cover/Interior Design & Layout: Petrafied Designs, LLC

ISBN-13 digit: 978-1-7339044-0-7

Library of Congress Control Number: 2019904917

All rights reserved. This book or any portion thereof may not be reproduced or used in any manner whatsoever without the express written permission of the publisher, except for brief and direct quotations in a book review.

To my sons, Ryan and CJ, and my Inner Circle: You inspire me. May we always choose to boldly and courageously live the lives of our dreams.

# **REIMAGINE** YOUR LIFE'S CAMINO

Whatever your age, gender, or life stage, do you sometimes feel like your life is whizzing by, yet not exactly as you'd imagined? Perhaps you feel a little bit stuck? Not sure how to get started redirecting your life's journey in a new direction? This book shares stories and lessons I've learned reimagining my path, or life camino.

As I see it, my life camino is my life journey where I travel a unique path through magnificent lessons, adventures, and experiences. As you read, you'll encounter the term life "camino-ing" which sounds more inviting and adventurous to me than life "path-ing."

The relatively recent shift along my own life's camino and the ongoing quest to reimagine my path has been heavily influenced by a pilgrimage through Spain known as "El Camino de Santiago," or "The Way of St. James". The Camino inspired many of the lessons captured here and changed my life in a way that no other experience has.

This book is dedicated to like-minded adventurers intent on evolving your life's camino and walking it your way. Here you'll find stories of a how a fellow camino-er transformed her life, along with inspiration to take action, and practical steps to shift your life's camino into high gear. This book is meant to be interactive. Please use it to write your thoughts as you read — as if we are walking and talking with one another.

Welcome to the Camino. You've found a fellow life explorer, and soon you'll discover your life camino tribe surrounding and supporting you at every turn. As we say in Spain to send good wishes to every traveler we meet along the path, "Buen Camino!"

# CONTENTS

## MY LIFE'S CAMINO — 1

## UNPACKING YOUR MIND — 5
Deal With Your Stuff — 7
Enough — 10
Commitment To Balance — 13
Routinize — 16
Baby Steps — 19
Time Stack — 22
Boundaries — 26
Share Your Truth — 29
Live Curiously — 32
Spontaneity — 35

## PACKING FOR THE JOURNEY — 38
Smart Travel Packing — 42
Travel Day Wear — 45
Capture The Moments — 48

## PREPARING TO STEP IT UP — 50
Body Tune Ups — 53
Wellness Check Ups — 56
Recharge Your Battery — 59
Financial Fuel — 63
Adjust Your Fuel Levels — 68
Low Octane Fuel — 71
High Octane Fuel — 77
Recycle — 82
Body Fuel — 85
Clean Your Tank — 88
Top Off Your Fluids — 91

## STEPPING ONTO THE TRAIL — 94
- Get Uncomfortable — 97
- Solo Prep — 100
- Pick Ups And Drop Offs — 104
- Merge Trails — 108
- Filters — 112
- Tune Your Radio — 115
- Crown Jewels — 118
- Travel Bingo — 121
- Sign Language — 124
- Navigation — 127
- Crossroads — 131
- Ask For Help — 135
- Slow Your Roll — 139
- Stop Littering — 142

## STOPPING ALONG THE WAY — 145
- Take a Break: Go Local — 148
- Mother Nature — 151
- Butterflies — 155
- The Doors — 158
- Oceans — 161
- Food Stops — 165
- Public Venues — 169
- Get After It — 174
- Holiday Traditions — 178
- Heart Gifts — 181
- Receiving — 184

## THE LAST WORD — 188

# MY LIFE'S CAMINO

The path to refocus my life's camino emerged in the early years of the 21st century, the year 2009 to be precise. Like all of us at times, I was stuck. I knew I hadn't been living the most authentic version of my life for some time. I was making myself sick with the inconsistency between living my life on other people's terms, for other people's needs and where I needed it to be: bigger, bolder, and more courageous.

The call to live a bigger, bolder life sprouted from the comfortable, predictable life I was living as a mother, a wife, a business executive, and an over-scheduled good friend. To the outside world, it looked like I had the ideal life. My family was healthy and behaving with kind manners toward one another. We shared laughter and good times with friends. My children were well adjusted and thriving. The bills were paid. We lived in a nice house, took great vacations, and had successful careers. While life was good, it felt like something was missing to me. Like there was more for me to be, more for me to explore, more for me to learn.

A bold leap of faith, a few steps in a new direction, and the transformation of my life's camino began. As I charged ahead, friends were inspired. The questions began: "How did you make this transformation happen?" and "How do I get what you have?" and "I want this. What steps did you take?" and, best of all, "Will you please put on paper what you just said so I can read it when I need a boost?"

The dream of a book was born. One that would help each of my tribe mates create the life of their dreams, to walk their own way on their own terms, in the midst of the magnificent chaos of everyday life.

For the past several years I've contemplated life's great mysteries while exploring the great outdoors and quaint, off-the-grid destinations near to home and around the globe. I've become more self-aware as I've processed important life lessons, and unpacked my thinking to let go of what was holding me back. This led to changes that made possible an energizing new way of life camino-ing.

Part of living on my own terms included opting out of a life-consuming corporate career and into a more flexible income-generating arrangement. I started a marketing consulting business with some business partners when I was 47 years old. That change created better balance and opened the door to new possibilities. Since then, I've found more time for life, lessons, and one of my great passions —

travel. I dreamed big and created opportunities to experience breathtaking locations from Machu Picchu, Peru to the Camino de Santiago in Spain to the Great Barrier Reef in Australia as well as many destinations in North America.

I dived into travel as a way to learn, grow, and recharge my spirit. Deliberately stepping it up in traveling the road ahead is an important metaphor for everyone's life journey. It's also likely one of the reasons I'm so passionate about travel. Trips and experiences in new places enliven my spirit. They remind me that I'm always exploring, evolving, and traveling my life's camino.

My life's camino, and the scenery surrounding it, change from moment to moment. Sometimes I'm walking a path that feels like a dirt road covered with brambles, barely passable. At times, it feels like I'm driving along a superhighway where I can put the pedal to the metal and speed along, completely free, with the wind whipping through my hair. Other times, I meet fellow travelers who ride or walk alongside of me for a time, changing speeds or turning a different direction, as their journeys evolve.

Here's how the Camino de Santiago figures into my story, with a bit of background for those new to the Camino. The Camino's purpose, since it was first created well over a thousand years ago, has been to provide pilgrims with the opportunity to contemplate their various transgressions and receive a pardon at the end of a very long walk. In modern times, a hodge-podge of travelers from countries the world over follow yellow arrows and seashell signage as they trek one of many official Camino routes to ultimately end the journey at the Cathedral in Santiago de Compostela, along Spain's northwest coast. Today pilgrims, or "peregrinos" as they are known on the Camino, make the trek for religious, spiritual, historic, cultural, and athletic reasons. According to the Pilgrim's Reception Office in Santiago, 278,232 walkers completed the journey in 2016. I was among those who walked the most popular route, the 500-mile (800-kilometer) Camino Frances from St. Jean Pied de Port, France in the Pyrenees Mountains to Santiago de Compostela, Spain.

For long walks across Spain, and those of everyday life, there are a number of actions that must be taken to prepare for the journey. Travelers need to unpack their thinking while packing their physical bags, prepare physically and financially to step onto the trail, and navigate unexpected twists and turns as they also enjoy various stops along the way. Each of these steps has the potential to teach important lessons if we pause to listen and welcome the messages meant for us.

The past few years of my life have centered on a transformation theme that taught me valuable lessons. May this book inspire you to think about your life, to dig deep, to take a few simple steps, and to boldly and unapologetically refocus your life's camino on your terms.

# UNPACKING YOUR MIND

Internal wiring drives thinking and therefore behavior. Life starts out simply enough as children, yet somehow as adults we end up overwhelmed with complicated, cluttered minds and lives. This section covers the most important shifts I made to begin transforming my life's camino. They primarily fall under the umbrella of simplification.

I discovered that before I changed what I did I needed to re-center and clean up my thinking to deal with mental barriers that held me back. There had to be a reconnection of my mind and heart so I could tap into my intuition and operate with all the tools available for my life journey.

Shifting my stride into high gear and living life on my own terms required that kind of a mental shift — a reconnection of mind and heart. Everyone is where they are because of the beliefs and thoughts they hold. Give the topics in this section a thorough review. You'll be miles ahead when, at the end of this book, you read suggestions about how you can make significant changes when you choose to do things and live life in different ways.

Contemplate which of your beliefs need to evolve so you can step up your life's camino and write them below:

What action steps will you take this week to begin making a shift?

As you make changes, you'll experience "a-ha!" moments of clarity. Use the space below to describe these moments and how it felt when they happened:

## DEAL WITH YOUR STUFF

"Stuff" is about tangible things, emotional baggage, and learned patterns that create mental programming. I needed to deal with all three aspects of "stuff" to shift my camino into high gear and start living the life of my dreams.

First was the tangible stuff. I needed to shift from collecting things to finding joy in life's everyday experiences. Sound familiar? You and I live in a world filled with over-consumption; too much food, and too many other things. Not enough simplicity and not enough gratitude.

Think about how this applies to your life by asking yourself the following question. "Would I rather have your presents or your presence?" These two words sound the same but mean very different things.

For a significant portion of life, I've watched many people as they've chased the presents. Striving for bigger paychecks, bigger houses, nicer cars, more clothes, better vacations and just more. The harder you charge after these things the more exhausted you become and the farther off track you feel.

You're probably familiar with the statistics. Over 70 percent of multi-million dollar lottery winners end up broke and file for bankruptcy. How is this possible? It happens day in and day out because even if you have more money than you'll ever need, materialism is its own form of addiction. Have more. Spend more. Want more. It's a never-ending quest.

As a senior executive working 24/7 for several large corporations, I chased the promotions and the perks. I had personal shoppers suggesting designer outfits and make-up artists primping me before presentations on stage. In a warped sort of way, it was fun to earn a promotion faster than someone else or be given a bigger raise or bonus than the year before. The faster I ran, the more exhausted I became.

A health crisis in my mid-40s changed my life and my thinking. It forced me to ask the hard questions of my inevitable mortality. What if this is it? What if I don't wake up tomorrow? Did I swing for the fences and live the life of my dreams or abdicate my dreams for the needs of others? Since I'm here a decade later, clearly I made it through the physical and emotional twists and turns of that stop along the journey. Presence versus presents. Thoughts versus things. Connections versus commercialism.

Contemplate where you have been, where you are now, and where you want to be on the presents versus presence spectrum. What action steps will you take this week to begin making a shift?

As you shift, you'll experience "a-ha!" moments of clarity. Capture them here in words:

## ENOUGH

As I moved away from "stuff," I poured through many books and YouTube videos in a quest for self-understanding and healing. Books and videos were (and are) an inexpensive, easy way to expose me to new thinking and challenge me to grow. When I recognized that I was caught up in material stuff, I asked, "Why?" A multitude of reasons flooded into my head, not the least of which was getting trapped in the endless loop of "not enough."

Several years ago, a good friend told me about Brené Brown's 2010 TedTalk on vulnerability, shame, and being enough. Back then Brené was an obscure academic and human connection researcher, not yet a best-selling author. With her 20-minute presentation (a conversation, really), Brené catapulted to fame ... which she shuns. I became a fan. She's authentic, funny in a humble, relatable way, and a role model for working on cleaning up what's held her (and all of us) back from greatness. She's dedicated her professional and personal life to understanding the dynamics of human behavior and how people are wired for connection. The why behind what we do. Whether she knows it or not she's philosophically part of the Life Camino tribe.

Brené has articulated better than anyone the insight that spawned what I call the "Enough Principle." As humans, we are wired for struggle. We worry and believe that we are not enough. On some level, we've convinced ourselves we aren't smart enough, thin enough, pretty enough, rich enough, fashionable enough, or successful enough. Because we don't remember that we are enough, we do crazy things like chase the collection of "more and better" tangible things.

Here's one of my favorite Brené quotes (from her TedTalk), wisdom that paved the path for a new approach to living my life's camino. These are words that you can take to heart and apply:

> *And the last, which I think is probably the most important, is to believe that we're enough. Because when we work from a place, I believe, that says, "I'm enough" ... then we stop screaming and start listening, we're kinder and gentler to the people around us, and we're kinder and gentler to ourselves.*

Watch the TedTalk. Thirty seven million viewers and counting have seen it and it's free. It's the best 20 minutes you'll invest this week even if you've seen it before. Take the inspiration further and pick up any of Brené's seven highly insightful books (as of 2019). My favorite is her 2010 bestseller, *The Gifts of Imperfection*.

Embracing vulnerability and truly believing I am enough and I have what I need altered the trajectory of my life. It's a mind space shift you too can embrace to jumpstart living the most joy-filled version of your life's camino.

**Contemplate whether there are times you also fall into the trap of believing you aren't enough. What action steps will you take this week to begin making a shift?**

_____

_____

_____

_____

**What were your "a-ha!" moments of clarity about believing that you're enough?**

_____

_____

_____

_____

## COMMITMENT TO BALANCE

I'm the type of person who's perpetually energized and loves to dive in. At times, I create an unintended tsunami effect on my life's camino. I can get so laser focused on what I'm doing that I lose perspective on everything else. If I'm writing a book, I can think of nothing else and I'm tied to my computer. If I'm trying to improve my tennis game, I play or practice five days a week. If I'm cleaning my house, I don't stop until every last crumb is swept up and there are no smudges left on any surface. When I was working, I was totally consumed by my corporate job. Even when I wasn't working, I was thinking about working. While the ability to have a laser focus is a great life skill that generates tremendous productivity, it can be, and usually is, exhausting. Ultimately it's not sustainable. It's unbalanced.

Some may not suffer from the overzealous, laser focused, "can't stop" version of the unbalanced disease, but rather the "too much relaxing and procrastinating" version of it. Are you the type of person who is perpetually talking about certain goals and aspirations yet never taking action on them? Wanting to quit a toxic job, lose several pounds, or exercise more, yet never seem to get around to it? This approach is also unbalanced and it's not serving your needs.

Job One is to step it up and shift your camino gears into motion. Be true to yourself and commit to whatever it is you want out of life. Honor that commitment by sticking with it and prioritizing time for it. The way I've been able to accomplish this is to start with a joy list. Not a toy list — a joy list! For several days in a row, spend a few minutes jotting down on a sheet of paper anything that comes to mind that makes you feel happy and joyful. Don't look at the list from the day before. Start a new list each day. Once you feel the lists get repetitive, go back through them and identify common themes. Choose the top three to five themes for which you feel the most passion. These core ideas become the priorities in which you begin to invest more time and energy. Keeping the list at three to five themes forces choices (priorities) and sets you up for success.

Contemplate in which areas your life's camino is not optimally balanced. What action steps will you take this week to begin making a shift?

___

___

___

___

___

___

These are some "a-ha!" moments as I saw myself shift:

___

___

___

___

___

___

## ROUTINIZE

Once you've committed to an action, weave it into the fabric of your day. The easiest way I've found to do this is to link it with a routine I've already established. This is the art of habit linking. I like to start my day with healthy actions and intentions. To keep me on track, I set up a routine: Drink a big glass of water, complete a five-minute plank exercise, make the bed, have a second glass of water, power walk for an hour with my neighbor. These five things are done every weekday with almost no thinking required on my part. I began with one action and after it became an established habit, I linked the other four actions. Routinized tasks are ones that get done.

There's a Part Two here, and it's about scheduling. Consider putting on the calendar anything you're committed to that is likely to consume 15 minutes or more that day. For example, I'll write events like walking with my neighbor, working out, lunches, business meetings, blocks of time for writing, time to call my kids, and going to a Spanish class. Everything I'm truly committed to doing is put into my calendar. Scheduling an activity makes it feel more like a meeting, and it elevates my commitment to doing it. Before you assume my calendar is overflowing with activities, let me assure you it's not. I set myself up for success by choosing a few things I truly want to accomplish. It doesn't matter if I meant to call my kids at 6:30 pm and it didn't happen until 7:30 pm — the important thing is that I commit to accomplishing things on my calendar at some point that day.

For activities that fall in the life maintenance category such as haircuts, doctor appointments, yard or garden service, it's easier for me to think about them once and then schedule them on a repeating basis. My hair and nail appointments are standing appointments, scheduled months in advance. It saves a huge amount of time and energy to approach it this way. Think about it. Doing it once and managing the exceptions is infinitely more efficient than dealing with thinking multiple times about needing to call for an appointment, getting voicemail, missing the return call, getting put on hold, etc. Do it once and be done with it.

Peter Drucker wrote, "What gets measured gets managed." My twist on this is, "What gets scheduled gets done." If I put an activity on my calendar there is a greater chance it will be accomplished today than if it's floating around in my head or even on a handwritten "to do" list. Schedule time each week for daily life maintenance items as well as three to five priorities and watch your productivity soar.

Contemplate the ways adopting routines or managing your calendar in a different way might help you transform your life's camino. What action steps will you take this week to shift?

Did you have a few "a-ha!" moments regarding a shift in routines or time management?

## BABY STEPS

I am living proof that consistent, persistent small steps yield massive results and put my life's camino on a completely different, and better, trajectory. Baby steps are a major reason I've made it to this point of living life on my terms.

I remember this lesson from my first life-changing trip along the Camino de Santiago. Embarking on this trek was a physical and mental challenge unlike any I had taken on previously. Like most things untried, I had some anxiety starting out. Would I get blisters from walking 15 to 18 miles, day after day? What if I couldn't keep up with my fellow pilgrims? I worried about staying in touch with friends and family back home and of being hopelessly lost in a remote village, not speaking a word of Spanish.

Two college-era friends of one of my consulting clients joined me on Camino. We stuck together as we got lost, shared our Camino experiences, and learned important life lessons. We began the first few mornings looking far into the distance saying things like: "Are you kidding me?

We need to make it all the way through this valley and over that mountain today?" My Camino buddies nicknamed me Dory after one of the fish in the movie "Finding Nemo." Remember the frequently repeated line "Just keep swimming?" We revised it while on the Camino to "Just keep walking." The three of us learned quickly to stop worrying, to stop looking too far ahead, and to focus on taking steps in the general direction of our destination. One step after another and before long we were there.

For those of you inspired by the idea of the Camino but without six weeks of free time to walk across Spain, start as I did. Watch the 2010 movie, "*The Way*," starring Martin Sheen. It's a great film that depicts one family's Camino story. The movie was my initial inspiration for this life-changing journey and it brings back great memories when I'm re-watching it.

There's magic that occurs with consistent, persistent effort, intentionally taking baby steps over and over again. Inspired and committed to transform your life? Dedicate just 15 minutes each day to an action that takes you one step closer to living life on your terms. It won't take long before you find yourself in a space that looks and feels completely new and different. You can find 15 minutes a day even if it means waking up earlier to do it. You and your dreams are worth it. Step up your camino and in the words of a favorite Nike slogan, "Just Do It."

Contemplate how your life's camino would be different with a commitment to consistent, persistent baby steps. What action steps will you take this week to begin making a shift?

"A-ha!" moments that arose from taking consistent, persistent baby steps:

## TIME STACK

Designing activities that accomplish multiple goals is an effective time management strategy. Time and money are limited commodities. When you're clear on your priorities, you have the opportunity to "time stack" them and accomplish multiple goals. For example, I enjoy playing tennis with a close friend and then catching up over an iced tea. This accomplishes exercise goals, feeds an important relationship connection, and costs next to nothing so I'm able to put away funds for other life experiences. Three goals accomplished via one activity.

Learn to be mindful during any multi-purpose activity. You'll miss the mark if you are distracted and not truly present. When playing tennis, I stay focused on the game and soak in every moment. When chatting with a friend, I engage fully and enjoy our connection. That means I'm not on social media, texting, or thinking about my next activity.

The concept of time stacking can be applied to every aspect of life from work, to socializing, to exercise, and to travel. What about time stacking when it's applied to travel and trip combinations? You've probably already tried a few of these ideas.

If you have limited paid time off work, take Fridays or Mondays to create long weekends. Two days off plus Saturday and Sunday doubles the fun. If you get to take a week off, leave as early as you can Friday after work and return a week from Sunday. This turns five vacation days into more than nine days of exploration. Time stacking in this situation is about maximizing time for soul enriching experiences while minimizing time away from daily responsibilities.

Another time stacking application I'm a huge fan of is business trip extensions. If your company sends you on an airplane somewhere for even a single day, there's an opportunity. The company is already paying for a flight, hotel, and other expenses related to the business trip so the costs added for extra time you can take for leisure are, by definition, less. Before you go, do some research on a travel website like TripAdvisor to identify the main sites in or near your business trip location. Then take an extra day to explore. You'll find an unexpected array of unique experiences that will stretch the "discoverer" in you. Companies can be flexible about travel days and won't insist you take an evening flight home after an afternoon meeting. Take a few hours to renew and recharge your battery.

For those feeling bad about being away from family due to a week or longer business trip, consider this an opportunity to practice your boundary management skills.

Overseas or not, longer duration trips provide even more opportunities to apply time stacking travel principles and create fantastic life experiences at low cost. If you need fly to another continent, fly during normal work hours (that's what they pay you to do). Schedule the trip so it's split between two workweeks with a weekend in the middle to explore the local sites, culture, and food. This is how I first explored the magic of Cuzco, Peru, and Machu Picchu. This approach works especially well the further from home you travel because companies benefit by avoiding the cost of multiple long distance flights and you benefit by managing jet-lag only once. Win-win.

Contemplate options for applying time-stacking principles in your life. What action steps will you take this week to begin making a shift?

Many "a-ha!" moment opportunities arise out of time stacking — what were yours?

# BOUNDARIES

As flight attendants remind us on every flight, "In the event of an emergency, please put on your own oxygen mask before helping others." At its core, this is a reminder to take care of yourself before you can truly be of service to others. This principle calls for mastering the art of simplifying your life by better setting personal boundaries. With a full array of work and family demands, you and I both know how tough this can be to put in practice.

Boundary management is one of life's great challenges. It's important to master in order to stay mindful as you create your new and improved life's camino. Sometimes, it can feel like you're expected to put your needs on the back burner and take care of everyone else first. As an adult, it's your job to change this mindset to support your desired way of living.

An observation: You train people how to treat you. Your actions show them what you are willing to accept and they behave accordingly by following the path of least resistance. It's true for pets, children, partners, and friends. The bottom line on boundaries is that you need to draw a line and say no. Say what you mean and mean what you say.

Time is a limited commodity that needs to be optimally managed to transform your life. Wasted time can never be recovered. Here's a somewhat fictionalized example from my life. A friend was perpetually late for lunch at a prearranged time. I was perpetually frustrated by this, and hungry. Instead of becoming annoyed and doing nothing about it, one time I waited five minutes past the appointed time, and then left. I sent a polite text and told her I was looking forward to rescheduling when it better worked with her schedule. It only took one time to draw the line and set the expectation. Natural consequences follow when you create or clarify a boundary. People learn that you mean what you say and will act accordingly.

Boundary setting is about honoring self. Make time for your needs, your life steps, and your dreams while still keeping the rest of your responsibilities humming along. Put this newfound time to use. Invest in you. You're likely to find far more than 15 minutes a day when you're disciplined about applying this principle. Once you've done this, set a goal to invest an hour a day "just for you" whether for a yoga class, working out, chatting with a friend, or reading a book.

Boundary management is responsible behavior; it's not selfish. You're teaching yourself and also other people important life skills such as how to be respectful, how to manage time, and how to get priority tasks done. These are great lessons for everyone.

Contemplate in which areas you most need to work on boundary management. What action steps will you take this week to begin making a shift?

Write the "a-ha!" moments that occurred around boundary management:

## SHARE YOUR TRUTH

One of the keys to living life on my terms is to own my truth and share it with others in a consistent and compassionate way. I grew up like many others of my generation, in a traditional household. It had both benefits and challenges. I thrived by not rocking the boat and keeping my opinions to myself. The programming that developed in me was equal parts pleaser and conflict avoider. More often than I'd care to admit, I failed to honor and share my truth. It took a significant amount of self-work to rewire this portion of my brain.

While avoiding conflict, I was also fiercely independent. I marched to the beat of my own drum and still do today. This was a positive outcome of being in the family that was mine. The ability to freely explore life without the undue influence of others led me to interesting people and career choices. Later in my career, I had the opportunity to work with the esteemed David TS Wood. He's a personal development guru, expert trainer of trainers, coach, and author. I credit him with opening my eyes to the importance of sharing my truth.

As professional colleagues, we attended numerous meetings and events together. I think about one of his mantras almost every day: "Tell the truth all the time with compassion."

His wisdom is a call to action to own what I think and feel, to put a voice to it, and to share it with others. At its core, it's about authenticity and self-accountability. "With compassion" is a critically important part of this life principle. Speaking my truth while being hurtful to others is not the way of living an enriching life camino. Speaking my truth with compassion sets the intention of honesty, helpfulness, and positivity. Beyond telling the truth or speaking the truth, I've become an advocate of sharing the truth. Sharing my truth adds the important element of connection. When I share something with another, it's part them and part me. It's a two-way street filled with potential for vulnerability and authentic communication.

Contemplate when and where you take opportunities to share your truth with compassion. What action steps will you take this week to begin making a shift?

Sharing truth with compassion lead to these "a-ha!" moments:

## LIVE CURIOUSLY

Along this winding life camino, I discovered the importance of living with curiosity. Being curious allows you to get to the essence of "what is." This non-judgmental way of being has the effect of opening your eyes to notice and appreciate nuances and differences that make the world special and unique. Let's face it. If everyone dressed the same, thought the same, believed the same, and had the same preferences, life would be as bland as plain oatmeal. Rolling with "what is" simplifies life, allowing you to live in the moment and experience the growth, learning, and joy you seek. It enables a curious mind that can appreciate the true colors, textures, and vibrancy of everyday life. It keeps walls down and puts you in an open, learning state of mind.

The second concept related to living curiously is a focus on asking questions that help you understand the world from a different point of view, or see it through a different filter. Being curious starts with thoughts like, "That's interesting," or, "I wonder ..."

"How is it possible to make that dye such a vibrant color naturally?"

"How did this culture come to have spiritual beliefs that are so different from mine?"

"How did people move those huge stones thousands of years ago to build that temple?"

Living in curiosity has enriched my life beyond measure. On a visit to Peru, it helped me immerse in the unique colors, textures, and fragrances of a local market. It connected me with a weathered and wise shaman whose market stall was filled with interesting objects. He told me of stories and rituals. I was able to truly appreciate the effort made by local weavers to create vibrantly colored dyes used to infuse color into hand woven blankets, capes, and scarves.

Today's world is brimming to overflow with divisiveness, anger, and judgmental reactions to different points of view on politics, religion, the education of children, the environment, and how to best manage healthcare. Everyone would benefit from taking a deep breath and being more curious. I see how different life can be when I go with "what is," and ask more questions … when I seek to understand versus when I condemn or criticize.

Contemplate when and where you most embrace living life with curiosity and wonder. What action steps will you take this week to begin making a shift?

What "a-ha!" realizations arrived when you focused on living with curiosity?

## SPONTANEITY

Planning, scheduling, list making, creating and following routines, and organizing just about anything is right up my alley. These skills come in handy for keeping my life on track. However, there's also so much magic in the unplanned that I have to write about spontaneity.

Some people are more naturally spontaneous than others. Usually, people less "wowed" by planning and structure have naturally stronger internal spontaneity meters. But, life can be richer if you embrace and encourage spontaneity in your life. As the consummate organizer, developing this skill took some practice. In trying to figure it out, I stumbled upon a couple of small steps that helped me re-wire my approach.

First, take daily actions that intentionally break a pattern of behavior. If you sleep on the right side of the bed, switch it up and sleep on the left side for a few days. If family members have designated spots at the dinner table, make it a norm that everyone chooses a different seat each meal. Take a different route to work or the grocery store. Ride a bike or walk to the bank instead of drive. There is a TedTalk by Terry Moore that explains a completely different (and better) way to tie your shoes. Learn to do this well-ingrained habit differently.

These are examples of things I do to shake things up and fuel the potential for spontaneity. Come up with your own ideas and make it a priority to approach several things differently each day. This small step has changed my perspective incredibly, energized my life, and paved the way for more spontaneity and fun.

A second thing I've done to increase spontaneity in my life was born through my work on a consulting project. Use an available container such as a Mason jar or a fishbowl. Write on small slips of paper some fun, no-cost or low-cost ideas of things you'd like to do but never seem to get around to. Set a maximum cost for each activity, especially if you have others helping you create the ideas, to avoid expectation issues down the road. Maybe you'll want to sample some horchata (a creamy tea-like drink), visit a flea market, sit in quiet and enjoy some wine while watching a sunset, find and cook a new recipe, or take a bike ride through a different part of town. Choose times to randomly pull an idea from the jar. These slips of paper identify your next spontaneous activity. Make a commitment to do this regularly and see how uplifted you feel. Add more slips of paper to the jar as you or family members brainstorm additional ideas.

Practicing the art of spontaneity brings more spice and fun to fully living your life's camino. It has impact far beyond the moment. It won't be long before even the most structured people loosen the chains a bit and seize the unexpected opportunities that present themselves.

**Contemplate how you can further develop your capacity for spontaneity. What action steps will you take this week to begin making a shift?**

_____

_____

_____

_____

**Living with more spontaneity led to "a-ha!" moments like these:**

_____

_____

_____

_____

# PACKING FOR THE JOURNEY

After mucking around unpacking my mind while learning to let go of limiting beliefs and patterns, it occurred to me that there is another type of tangible action important to the success of my reimagined journey. This section deals with learning to prepare and re-pack smartly for the journey ahead.

There's an art to packing for life camino adventures. It's definitely not celebrity style with serious travel wardrobes, huge trunks, satchels, train cases, and roller bags. It's about simplifying and minimizing what I carry to focus on experiences not the clothes on my back or the knick-knacks in my home.

When I asked myself why I hold onto the things I do, it's often difficult to answer. If you're like me perhaps you'd say, "It's perfectly good stuff, why get rid of it? As soon as I do, I'll need it." Holding onto things for sentimental reasons is common: "The cute artwork my child created for me 20 years ago, along with every short story and drawing made throughout his school years is adorable, so how can I throw them away?" Holding onto things for what seem like practical reasons is common: "I might need that pair of jeans later if I gain or lose weight." And, holding onto things might just be neglect: "I'm simply too busy to deal with the clutter accumulating in my house." There are a million reasons why release is a challenge.

As a member of this first world society overburdened by excess and too many storage units, I know firsthand that clutter is draining our collective energy and consuming precious time at unprecedented levels. I hadn't considered the fact that every item in my house requires space, plus my time to dust it, clean it, or file it. It's common to look at the mail, move it to a pile, and shuffle through it again later. The cycle repeated until eventually I took action. Each time I looked at the mail or an email and left it to deal with later, I choose to spend time re-engaging my brain cells on it a second, third, or fourth time.

I attended a seminar on the topic of handling everything once and immediately putting it in its place. I learned there about the "5-S" philosophy of life, which is of Japanese origin. The five "s" words are seiri, seiton, seiso, seiketsu, and shitsuke. These words translate to the definition of a commitment to order, cleanliness, and purity. How does it work? Look at the mail and pay the bill or toss the junk mail in the trash as soon as it's brought into the house. Put the sheets in the washer and dryer and then immediately back on the bed. Don't move the sheets to a temporary pile and work on something else. Finish the task, and put the item in its place. Get into a mind space where everything has a designated storage location and is easy to find. This way of life eliminates buying multiples of the same item in the way a single pair of scissors that's stored where you know you'll find them is enough.

I'd implemented a few 5-S principles in my home life when a good friend recommended a book titled: *The Life-Changing Magic of Tidying Up: The Japanese Art of Decluttering and Organizing,* by Marie Kondo. Her Kon-Mari method is now so popular, there's a Netflix series about it. Marie gives step-by-step instructions to unpack your life.

At the end of this uncluttering process, I was energized. I felt physically lighter. There were multiple large black Hefty trash bags with items ready to move out of my space. To be honest, I still have boxes of my kids' artwork in the garage. However, most of the inside of my house is clutter-free and has remained that way for over a year. Removing what you no longer need, and organizing your space are two exercises well worth your time.

Contemplate changes you can make to simplify your life by tidying up. What action steps will you take this week to begin making a shift?

Describe the "a-ha!" moments you felt when your life's camino got more simple and clean:

## SMART TRAVEL PACKING

Living a renewed life camino is about experiences, not things. You can only bring so much on the journey. Regardless of your trip's mode of transportation, you need to make smart packing choices. My life packing philosophy is "think carry-on," let go of the need for designer options, and travel light.

A key difference with packing light versus other packing styles is options management. My travel friends and I laugh about the fact that I bring the smallest suitcase and almost never check luggage. We take pictures of our group's combined luggage to document the quantum differences in our approach. Even for long weekends, some of my friends bring multiple bags packed full of clothes, shoes, and accessories. I bring a carry-on suitcase that's only half-full.

Looking and feeling fabulous is fun. Everyone wants to look great. The major difference with my minimalist packing approach is having a wardrobe plan for the most likely activities, not multiple options for each activity. I let go of the opportunity to decide on the spot which of three outfits to wear to an event. There's no thinking involved at the destination, just one pre-determined option. I choose basics I can mix and match, to dress an outfit up or down as the situation requires, and I'm comfortable with wearing the same outfit more than once.

When you pack light, you don't need to check bags on airline flights. Carry-on bags save both time and money. Having observed this hundreds of times, waiting at the baggage claim adds a minimum of thirty minutes to travel time. That's an hour per trip of limited "me" time to reinvest better in your life's camino.

Carry-on bags keep you in control of your belongings. While over 95 percent of the time airlines get checked bags to the correct baggage claim carousel upon arrival, do you really want to be part of the five percent standing in line at customer service because of a lost bag?

If traveling for a month or more, check a roller bag as your best option. Most airlines mandate that checked bags weigh less than 50 pounds; go over and be charged an excess weight fee. Even when checking a bag, you have to think about packing smart.

Throughout my first five-week, 500-mile Camino trek through Spain, I lived out of a roller bag limited to 40 pounds. It was moved from hotel to hotel each day so that I could walk seven hours carrying only a light daypack. In addition to walking attire basics, I packed two cute dresses and a pair of flat sandals. I wore one of these two outfits to dinner each night for five straight weeks. The dresses made me feel feminine and energized me after wearing trail runners and hiking shorts all day. No one else had packed a dress and not a single person seemed to notice that I wore the same outfit over and over. Re-use and re-wear felt so good.

Contemplate your typical approach to travel packing. What changes might you make to lighten the load for your next trip? Are there items you typically over pack that you can let go of? Are there items you might add to your travel inventory that will help simplify packing? What action steps will you take to begin making a shift?

_____

_____

_____

Write some "a-ha!"s about packing light for travel:

_____

_____

_____

## TRAVEL DAY WEAR

There are several schools of thought regarding what to wear en-route to a destination whether you're walking, in the air, on a train, or in a car. It's a tough balance between looking good, feeling comfortable, and optimizing suitcase space.

Comfort wins. I go with yoga pants or leggings every time. Everyone needs one or more comfy outfits for exercise and relaxation. For many women this consists of yoga pants, a tee shirt, a long-sleeved sweater or jacket, and tennis shoes. Beyond comfort, these layers create options for managing unpredictable, but often colder than expected, temperatures en route. This type of clothing is comfortable for more than a few hours, upping the odds you'll arrive at your destination a bit more rested. Walking through airports, catching cabs, and maneuvering luggage to your hotel room are all more easily managed in sneakers. Hand carrying the bulky winter jacket or sweatshirt you'll need saves suitcase space and keeps it easily accessible.

You may also want to consider the strategic use of a comfy fleece headband. For about $25, fleece headbands embedded with Bluetooth speakers are a great travel investment. You can use them for listening to music, watching a movie, blocking out light to get some rest, and for creating a visible barrier that discourages nearby passengers from chatting with you.

Chatting and networking have their place, but on a multi-hour flight, my goal is to rest so I can hit the ground running and take in the sights at my destination. Put your headphones on as soon as the flight is in the air and people will rarely interrupt you (they can't tell if you are or are not listening to music, a podcast, an audiobook, whatever). Close your eyes and rest, read a book, or write in your journal. Feeling social? Pop the headband off for a while, and chat with your seatmate if it feels right.

Contemplate optimizing your travel day clothing strategy. What action steps will you take to begin making a shift?

Write at least one "a-ha!" awakening about clothing on travel days:

## CAPTURE THE MOMENTS

Most cell phones come with cameras these days. I always have my iPhone camera with me. Not long ago, I purchased a mirror-less Sony camera with detachable lenses to enhance the artistry of photos and to give me the option of printing them in larger sizes. If you're planning to look at your photos online, or print them in size 5 x 7 or smaller, a mobile phone camera is really all you need.

Besides the inherent "wow" factor that comes from capturing a stunning sunset photo or snapping a picture of a majestically perched butterfly, photography has opened up a new way for me to experience the world. First, it trained my eye to notice the small details I used to ignore. It also changed my life perspective by encouraging me to look at situations from different angles.

One of my friends is a photography expert and taught me what we call The Ten-Step Game. Choose a starting point and snap 50 unique pictures within ten steps in any direction. Crouch down, turn around, and look up. Intentionally examine the scene from many different angles. Download these pictures to your computer to identify the best shots and delete those that don't speak to the artist in you. I especially love this activity when traveling solo. It gives me something interesting to stay busy with and prompts me to notice the little things along my life's camino.

**Contemplate new ways to use your camera phone in a new location to see the world through a new lens. What action steps will you take this week to begin making a shift?**

---

---

---

---

**Come up with an "a-ha!" idea or two about using your cell phone's camera:**

---

---

---

---

# PREPARING TO STEP IT UP

As a fan of physical movement, it's difficult for me to sit still for long. I most enjoy moving the old fashioned way, using my two feet. The best motivational tool I've integrated into my wellness routine is a fitness tracker. There are many good affordable brands. It's not the latest version but I love my Fitbit Charge 2. I use it to track the number of steps I've taken each day and to monitor my sleep quality. Priced at $125, it's an investment that pays for itself in smart ways.

I got on the Fitbit bandwagon in summer of 2016, before my first trip along the Camino de Santiago. My travel mates and I ordered Fitbits and tracked our training walks so we could compare progress and motivate each other while looking forward to the "long walk" across Spain. Since then, I've walked over 12 million steps. That's more than 5,400 miles (8,700 kilometers).

Remember: What gets measured gets done. Set a daily goal to "step things up" in your life. A healthy goal is 10,000 steps per day. Being able to check my step numbers throughout the day makes me think about parking further away from the grocery store entrance, taking the stairs versus the elevator, and not missing morning walks.

If you lived in Europe, you'd be more accustomed to walking everywhere. Many healthy eating and lifestyle approaches, like the Mediterranean diet, leverage walking as an important factor. Whatever goal you set for a step number per day, come up with a general plan for how you're going to achieve it so it's not 8:00 pm and you're still 6,000 steps from your goal. Walking for an hour at a steady pace generates about 6,000 steps. Playing doubles tennis for two hours logs around 5,000 steps. Another way to build steps into your daily routine is to walk at lunch or between meetings on workdays. Find Meet-Up groups and free local walking tours where you have the opportunity to visit another side of town or interact with people who have walking as a common interest.

Contemplate ways you can step it up in your daily life. What action steps will you take this week to begin making a shift?

One of my friends has this motto: "Walking solves everything!" What's your "a-ha!" about stepping up your exercise plan?

## BODY TUNE UPS

Walking is great but it's insufficient for optimal health. Everything I've read reinforces the importance of strength training several times a week, in addition to cardio and aerobic exercise. Walking 30 minutes per day counts as cardio and/or aerobic exercise.

You don't need to pay $50 to $70 per hour for a personal trainer. If you've never worked out with weights before it's best to consult with your doctor to make sure you choose a plan suited for you. While it's possible to learn everything you need to know on the internet, I found it best to work out with a trainer for a few months so I could learn how to do the exercise routines and stay in proper form for safety. Now it's easy to manage strength training with a small amount of home gym equipment and redirect the funds for a personal trainer to other experiences on my life's camino.

Three steps I've incorporated to keep me going on my workout regimen are:

1) Having a friend to work out with — a great way to build self-accountability and keep motivation high;

2) Searching online for routines I can do in my home workout area. There are workouts for upper and lower body, push/pull exercises, and targeted body part workouts (biceps, abs, hamstrings) that are easy to follow; and

3) Accepting "30 day challenges" I find on Google — where there are challenges for exercises like squats and planks to complete exactly as shown or to modify. I switched up a squats challenge from 30 to 60 days. Then I switched to a planks challenge and worked my way up to five-minute planks each day. None of these body tune-up activities require a trainer.

What inspires you? Take your exercise routine outdoors. Visit parks, playgrounds, hiking trails. Put on a helmet and inflate your bike's tires. See how many miles you can ride in an hour. Walk the neighborhood or go for a jog. Train for a half-marathon or a five-kilometer run if you like feeling your feet pound the pavement. All of these activities cost nothing. Or, you can choose to invest less than $100 in items like a yoga mat, some resistance bands, an exercise ball, and a couple of medium-sized free weights for your home workout space. You don't need a fancy gym. You can work out in a spare bedroom or even a modestly sized walk-in closet. Set your workout equipment in view so you'll notice it and be encouraged to get in a few reps a few times a week.

Contemplate ways you can incorporate strength training and other forms of physical activity into your daily life's camino. What action steps will you take this week to begin making a shift?

Take a deep breath, and write some "a-ha!"s about how exercise benefits you:

## WELLNESS CHECK UPS

To be fully prepared for life's camino, occasionally everyone needs to be checked out by a professional. I'm a huge believer in completing screening tests on the schedules for which they're recommended. Whether it's a colonoscopy, a mammogram, a dental cleaning, or routine blood work, taking the time to visit health professionals to ensure systems are running smoothly is well worth the effort and cost. A problem identified early can be treated quickly with minimal downtime. Life-changing health problems occur when you knew there was something going on and did nothing; or, you felt fine and were "too busy" to schedule the annual physical.

I've had oddball test results and a surgery or two to remove a something that shouldn't have been there. I'm in excellent health, and able to live my dream life camino because I am proactive and don't wait for health situations to get out of control. Financially, it's smart to handle health situations early. There are minimal medical costs for minor issues. Major medical costs for major issues mean a large diversion of time and funds from one's life camino priorities.

Even more important to me than traditional doctors and hospitals are nature-based health practitioners. My naturopath was the health professional that figured out why I was feeling exhausted when those in the traditional medical community missed it. While I'm on the "natural" bandwagon, here's my best advice: Take plant-based nutritional supplements versus pharmaceuticals, and visit massage therapists, chiropractors, and acupuncturists to stay tuned up. Wellness and prevention are keys to healthy and happy longevity.

Contemplate new ways to incorporate wellness checkups into your routine to ensure your body is tuned up for your life's camino. What action steps will you take this week to begin making a shift?

_____

_____

_____

_____

What "a-ha!" moments did you experience regarding your plan to stay physically healthy?

_____

_____

_____

_____

## RECHARGE YOUR BATTERY

Restorative deep sleep leads to the best feelings on waking. I can fall asleep with ease and stay asleep for nine or ten hours. Not everyone has this natural ability. It has something to do with the perpetual motion wavelength I operate on … and, I discovered there's another reason.

I always thought I was a great sleeper because I could sleep so many hours day after day, or fall asleep on a crowded tour bus. But, a mild case of sleep apnea kept me from actually getting any restorative deep sleep, and Rapid Eye Movement (REM) sleep, where most dreaming occurs. If you're constantly tired, you can't recall your dreams, or if your partner tells you the entire neighborhood can hear your snoring, you might want to check into whether you have sleep apnea.

Sleep apnea is just one sleep issue. There are many problems people experience with sleep, from untreated chemical imbalances in the brain where a person's mind won't shut off, to waking up in the middle of the night after only a couple hours sleep, to not being able to fall asleep in the first place. There is arguably nothing worse for your health than continuous sleep deprivation, running on empty day in and day out. Beware of using medications to sleep; they can create addiction and also interact with other medications. Be sure to discuss any and all medicines you use for sleep and other health challenges with your doctor, including dietary supplements, to ensure you have the proper regimen for your needs.

I'm a fan of planning for eight hours of sleep without the use of sleep aids. My battery recharging routine also includes five to ten minutes of stretching and simple yoga poses each morning, going to an occasional restorative (yin) yoga class, and sitting quietly listening to the birds on my patio over a cup of coffee. Part of living life on my terms includes proactively finding time to exhale. And to breathe deep.

Many people enjoy journaling. When the mood strikes me, I use a gratitude journal. In the morning, I set my intention for the day and write down three things I'm grateful for. This takes less than five minutes. When I'm not writing in a journal, I often make a mental list, and challenge myself to avoid repeating the same themes. I am eternally grateful for my sons, my family, and my friends. I make my statements specific which seems to unlock more happiness and joy. Writing helps me process my life lessons and clarify how I feel about people or situations without the influence of anyone else's point of view. It helps me recharge my battery and keep my life's camino on track. If writing isn't your thing, consider downloading some meditation podcasts and take the time and space to listen and participate.

To fuel your life transformation, figure out the rituals and activities that renew your spirit. Take time for them each and every day.

Contemplate new approaches to recharge your battery. What action steps will you take this week to begin making a shift?

What are your "a-ha"s regarding the ways in which you recharge your battery?

## FINANCIAL FUEL

Before embarking on the next phase of life camino-ing it's important to establish fuel reserves. Handling resources effectively is what enhances how much and how well you experience life. Learning to shepherd my financial resources effectively made a step-change difference in the quality of my life's camino. Managing financial fuel must come first.

If you hired someone to show you how to update your wardrobe, the first thing they'd do is assess its current state. They'd spend time with you while you tried on your clothes. They'd look at what you have, what doesn't work for you any longer, and talk about how you'll use what's left. Afterwards you'd be in a position to figure out your wardrobe gaps and come up with a plan and make priorities to fill them.

Getting your spending organized is no different. I had no idea what I was spending money on when I was married, working full time, and busy with two kids. When I decided I wanted to move my life's camino in a new direction, it gave me the motivation to figure out a money management system that works for me. I'm able to create my dream life with far fewer funds than I ever imagined by focusing on my priorities and eliminating wasteful spending. To accomplish this, I needed to understand my spending patterns.

Not everyone loves numbers, spreadsheets, and math. I understand. That said, just because you don't prefer something is no excuse to avoid it. There's a feeling of security that comes from knowing how many funds are coming in and how many are going out. I'm a frugal person because I grew up in a family that always had enough, but not a lot. We were practical. We saved for a rainy day. We ate tuna noodle casserole. We didn't visit restaurants except on birthdays. We drove to nearby Wisconsin for summer vacation to visit grandma and cousins. This early financial programming came in handy once I focused on a goal of retiring early while still being able to fund my dream lifestyle.

Are you sabotaging your dreams by coming up with excuses that allow you to behave in a financially lazy manner? Whether you were born with healthy financial wiring or not, all you really need to do is choose to shift now. What's the best way to get financially organized? The answer to that question is: "Whatever way you are going to stick with."

To start fully living your life's camino you simply must invest some time in planning and organizing your spending.

That means developing an annual budget, tracking what's happening, and adjusting along the way. If you're not a computer person, that's fine too. This process has been managed on paper for centuries.

The easiest way I've found to manage my financial fuel is to create a monthly budget and electronically download bank account, credit card, and debit card information into an excel file. I think of credit card charges as if they were made on a debit card. This means the credit expense should be added to your tracking system as soon as the item is purchased. Live within your means and pay off the credit card debt in full every month. Write checks instead of using cash to avoid the extra mental effort associated with keeping track of where the cash goes.

One money management author who inspires me is Dave Ramsey. He wrote *The Total Money Makeover: Classic Edition: A Proven Plan for Financial Fitness.* He's direct and has good suggestions for getting financial fuel under control.

If you need a tracking system that's already set up and you have a computer, the program named Quicken is a user friendly, inexpensive, and time proven software package that functions like the Excel model I use (Quicken works on PC and Mac products). It takes a couple of hours to learn the system and get things rolling but once you do, it's easily updated in less than 30 minutes per month.

If you're not a computer aficionado, here's an easier way to start. Get a handle on your last full calendar month's expenditures to establish a baseline. Collect and compile the receipts or downloaded summaries. Categorize each expense using standard budget categories. You probably won't remember details, and that's OK. Look at ATM withdrawals and see how much cash you're burning through. Categorize the cash expenses. This will be the most challenging part. Seriously, cash just evaporates. Total up similar expenses.

If looking back seems unmanageable, yet another way to start is a forward-looking approach. For the next month keep every receipt and write the expense category on it. Store these receipts in a large envelope. Every time you use cash, make a note of the amount and category on your calendar. The point is to get a handle on how much is spent in which categories. This way you have the knowledge and power to make decisions about reallocating more funds toward fun choices and less toward daily life expenses. It doesn't have to be perfect. Just get started.

Contemplate how you feel about your financial fuel. What changes might you benefit from making? What action steps will you take this week to begin making a shift?

Financial fuel is an area of life where "a-ha!"s are necessary. What are yours?

## ADJUST YOUR FUEL LEVELS

I kept up with budgets and tracking. The process became easier, less time consuming, and honestly, it got a bit tedious as time went on. I like competitions and puzzles. I felt like I needed to "game-ify" my financial fuel management process to make additional progress.

Here's how this works. Divide expenses into two mega-categories. "Low Octane" expenses are daily life expenditures for things like mortgage/rent, phone, utilities, car, gas, or health care. Low octane funds keep the lights on in daily life. "High Octane" expenses relate to experiences and fun; things like food (restaurant meals or prepared at home), sports/fitness activities, vacations, or clothes. The objective of the game is to maximize funds in the High Octane category.

Budget lines can be allocated to either category depending on how they make you feel. Perhaps owning the most incredible home in town is worth every penny of the expensive mortgage that goes with it. If this is true for you, it belongs in the High Octane category. For me, a hefty mortgage focuses on things versus the experiences I'd rather have. Housing costs are in the Low Octane category in my budget.

As for winning the octane game — High and Low — here's how it works. Maximize and grow the percentage of High Octane funds. Over four years, I've reduced Low Octane expenses to 37 percent and increased High Octane spending to 63 percent of my budget. When I started down this path, the percentages were nearly reversed. The radical shift from about 40 percent to 60 percent in high octane spending represents thousands of dollars per year more for life camino-ing without any change in my income. It's motivating to see how much freedom you can have when you make different daily choices with your time and monetary resources.

Contemplate how you allocate your financial fuel. How much is Low Octane versus High Octane? What action steps will you take this week to begin making a shift?

Did any High or Low Octane "a-ha!"s come your way with this shift?

## LOW OCTANE FUEL

Here are some of the Low Octane changes I made. It may give you some concrete ideas and an idea of the magnitude of what's possible to get your own fuel optimization process started. My specific choices are unimportant. This process about making choices that will work for you in accelerating your life camino transformation.

Let's start with some perspective that changed my financial thinking. To put the concept of small steps into financial terms, consider this. Financial investment professionals say that if a person shaved just $100 a month in expenses and invested it every month for 10 years, at the end of that time their bank account balance would be over $18,000. Depending on the financial assumptions, that's $12,000 in savings and $6,000 in investment gains without having to lift a finger. Regardless of the exact math, this represents significant funds to reallocate to retirement or to your High Octane activities.

I asked myself, "What if I could eliminate $100 per month in Low Octane spending?" I quickly calculated $100 per month for 12 months is $1,200. That's half a vacation for a single traveler. While it can be a bit more challenging with additional family members in the financial mix, there's also a lot more than $100 per month in savings potential with a group. Get the other family members on board. Ditch today's lazy spending habits to start funding and living your dream life camino.

These Low Octane adjustments had the biggest impact on fueling my High Octane funds: I chose to reduce cable TV and saved $100 a month. I wasn't watching much TV, certainly nowhere near the number of channels I was paying for. I turned off the television and began to enjoy the great outdoors or read a book. I added Netflix and Hulu (less than $10/month). This provides plenty of options to address my occasional need for a movie or TV fix. Besides saving money, this change freed up several hours per day for higher priority life camino activities.

Ditch the landline for savings of $15 and up to $35 per month. Landlines have gone the way of the dinosaur. Even my elderly parents have cell phones, as did my children from sometime in middle school. Landlines, and their expenses, are completely unnecessary. If you feel the need for a home phone line, at a minimum get a Magic Jack that runs off your internet service and port your landline telephone number over to it. This will still save more than 80 percent on your bill.

Take on some household chores to save between $150 and $300 per month. Do you have a housekeeper or landscaping crew a couple of times per month? Their services are convenient but the costs add up. Consider cutting back on frequency or getting the family involved and do the work yourself. I split the difference. I clean my house, but use a landscaper to keep the yard and trees looking good.

Adjust the temperature on your thermostat. Savings: $20 to $80 per month. Three degrees warmer in the summer and three degrees cooler in the winter saved a surprising amount on my utilities bill. If you're living in a bigger place than you truly need with multiple heating and air conditioning units, consider moving to a smaller place where even more savings are possible. Relatedly, turn off the lights and unplug electronics when not in use.

Join utilities saver plans. Savings: $15 to $25 per month. Shift utility consumption to off-peak hours, typically evenings after 8 pm and weekends. These are the hours you're typically home from work so this switch requires minimal behavior change.

Buy gasoline from Club stores. Savings: $12 to $25 per month. I buy virtually all of my gasoline at Costco. If you aren't already a member, gasoline savings alone will cover the cost of membership. More savings are possible from shifting to lower octane fuel (just in this one case!) Regular unleaded gas has an octane level of 87 while premium has 91. Those four octane points add more than 10 percent to the price. Unless you're driving a Lamborghini (and even then) your car will not notice the difference.

Wash the car(s) yourself. Savings: $10 to $30 per month. Get the kids involved and splash around in the driveway the old fashioned way.

Sign up for Ebates. Savings: $25 or more per month, depending on your shopping habits. Ebates is a game changer for maximizing online shopping discounts. Ebates gives members access to constantly changing low percentage rebates on most purchases from most retailers. This is in addition to points or cash back you may already earn with your credit card. After signing up for your free Ebates account each time you shop online start at the Ebates website or add the automatic browser extension. Click on a button to activate a shopping trip with your desired retailer and make your purchase through the retailer's shopping cart process using your usual payment method.

Borrow versus buy printed materials. Savings: $50 per month. The savings here depends on how much of a reader you are. If you buy novels, magazines, newspapers, and the like fairly often, you know that once they're read, they create clutter. Borrow them from the library instead. Library cards are free. Everyone should have one.

Use free library "Culture Passes." Savings: $30 per month. Libraries offer much more than books for borrowing. Additional offerings include movies, music, and access to museums or other cultural activities. Free "Culture Passes" for two guests to many local venues are available for checkout. Museums, botanical gardens, and tours are accessible at no cost. Spend an afternoon somewhere you wouldn't normally visit. It's a great way to practice spontaneity and save money.

The cumulative effect of these simple changes gave me an additional $400 each month to redirect to fun soul-enriching experiences, four times my initial "what if" goal. What would you do with an extra $4,800 every year in High Octane fuel? I invest much of these 'saved' funds on travel. You can choose to spend it all on a week traveling to some exotic destination or spread it over more frequent smaller trips. Consider allocating funds for classes in one of your priority interest areas. That could include things like learning a foreign language, photography classes, or cooking lessons. What's on your life's camino priority list that these funds could jumpstart?

Contemplate ways you can let go of wasteful spending on Low Octane expenses. How much of an impact could this have on building your High Octane fuel reserves? What action steps will you take this week to begin making a shift?

___

Some "a-ha!"s about saving-to-spend-for-fun were:

## HIGH OCTANE FUEL

Mental laziness about financial fuel held me back from living the life of my dreams much more than the actual funds I had available. Focusing and treating my financial fuel with respect unlocked a vast number of High Octane life experiences that were once outside of my paradigm. How will you focus, with respect, on your financial fuel?

High Octane expenses have many optimization opportunities. I discovered some relatively painless opportunities to redirect spending into areas that brought me more joy.

Drop the coffee shop habit. Savings: $50 to $100 per month. Many people have a routine where they drop by Starbucks or Dutch Bros. for a morning caffeine fix. I used to be one of them, and, sometimes I'd stop for an afternoon pick-me-up as well. These favorite sugary, dairy-filled concoctions can cost upwards of $5 each. Invest in a Nespresso coffeemaker or a Keurig with refillable pods. You'll save money, not to mention precious time waiting in line that can be re-invested in more enjoyable life camino activities.

Eat before you leave home. Savings: $50 to $100 per month. Breakfast is the easiest meal of the day to prepare. A bowl of cereal, yogurt, toast, juice, a bagel with cream cheese, and even scrambled eggs are simple enough for even beginner cooks to whip up at a fraction of the cost of eating out. The average on-the-go breakfast burrito or egg sandwich costs between $4 and $6. Breakfasts out for 20 workdays a month? Do the math!

Reinvent grocery shopping. Savings: $100 per month. As a single shopper, it took some time to fully crack the code on shopping for food and supplies. Club store quantities for most items outside of paper goods overfilled my pantry. If I loaded up at the grocery store, I ended up with spoiled produce a week later. Consider stocking up on protein at Costco. These items offer the biggest savings versus similar items at a grocery store. Much of their meat and fish selection is organic and costs several dollars per pound less. Once home, I repackage the items into individually portioned Ziploc bags, Sharpie the date on the bag, and freeze them. Two slices of bacon, four ounces of frozen shrimp, pre-sliced veal saltimbocca, or chicken, one Italian sausage, or one steak each go into its own Ziploc bag. When I'm ready to cook, I grab as many portions as I need for that meal. My grocery stops are quick because I typically don't need much more than fresh produce for the recipes I'm cooking that day. Plant an herb garden for even more savings!

Maximize grocery store discounts. Savings: $100 per month. The digital version of couponing is right up my alley. Download the app for your favorite grocery store and sign up for a loyalty card. Grocery stores offer better pricing and sales for loyalty card members. If you're over 55, there's typically a day each week or month they offer an additional 10 percent or more savings. In-app coupons and in-store deals can easily be linked to your loyalty card. When you purchase a sale item using your loyalty card, the discounts are automatically applied to your total.

Make eating out count. Savings: $200 to $300 per month. If you eat lunch at a casual restaurant every workday, it's likely you are spending at least $15 a day doing so. Many decisions to eat out are the result of lack of planning. It takes so little time to put together a sandwich with a piece of fruit or to pack up dinner leftovers for lunch the next day. I limit eating in restaurants to once a week and make it a special event, a lunch or dinner that I can enjoy with a friend.

My efforts here yielded more than twice as many funds as the earlier Low Octane process did with a total of $1,100 per month saved for life camino-ing. That's $13,200 over the course of a year. Add that to the $4,800 in Low Octane savings and that's $18,000 per year in life camino funds from simple alterations to spending habits.

If you're the type of person who benefits from keeping funds in separate accounts to avoid the temptation to spend what's in front of you, set up a High Octane savings account and transfer these funds to it before you pay a single bill. The better your skills develop in the areas of budgeting and tracking, the more confidence you'll have in spending to your limits in the various areas. Do this however it works best for you.

Contemplate ways you can reprioritize spending to grow your High Octane fund for spending in areas that truly bring you joy. What action steps will you take this week to begin making a shift?

What are your High Octane "a-ha!"s?

## RECYCLE

What do you do with perfectly usable items in the multiple black Hefty garbage bags you filled by doing the tidying up exercise? A proverb from the 17th century: "One person's junk is another person's treasure," is a truth that has been known for centuries. Recycling and re-using are great ways to protect the environment and lighten your personal load.

There's sometimes even a financial fuel opportunity in recycling. How many things do you buy that you end up barely using? Stop buying clothing that will only hang in the closet. You don't need the latest gadget to make cleaning or organizing easier. Only purchase books you plan to read starting the day you buy them. Unused items waste money, and they get in the way of your desire to feel free so recycle them by donating to charity or to recycling centers.

Tap into consignment shops. Savings: $100 and more per month. Upscale kids', men's, and women's clothing consignment shops, as well as re-sale stores featuring furniture and decorative accessories have popped up across the U.S. Take gently used items to one near where you live and see what they'd be willing to sell them for on your behalf. Generally, proceeds are split equally with the seller. These funds can be cashed out or used to buy items from that store for your home or family members. The shop owner or staff may donate to charity what you brought that didn't sell and give you a donation slip for it.

Sell items on Offer Up. Savings: It depends. This is a great app for selling bigger ticket items such as barbecue grills, appliances, and bicycles. It's worth it to give it a try before making a Goodwill run because fairly priced items can sell in a matter of hours.

Contemplate changes you can make to simplify your life and at the same time amp up your efforts to re-use and recycle to help preserve the planet. What action steps will you take this week to begin making a shift?

Did you have a few "a-ha!" moments with regard to recycling?

## BODY FUEL

Food is a touchy subject because while it is fuel, it's about much more than providing your body with the appropriate number of calories. It's about connecting and celebrating. It's a form of entertainment, a social environment for good times spent with family or friends. It conjures up memories of home cooked comfort food. It's a fast food crutch for dealing with the time pressures of your daily schedule. It's a tool to manage fear of not having enough. It fills a person's tank that's empty of emotion. It eases boredom and seems to cure longing. Food is linked to many aspects of life beyond calorie consumption.

When I started down my new life camino path a few years ago, I was 40 pounds overweight despite working out several times a week. While I live an active lifestyle, I learned quickly that weight is mostly driven by the food I consume. I was regularly filling my tank with non-nutritious junk food and eating mindlessly in a race to get to the next task on my to-do list. I started eating "clean," tracked my food intake, and lost those 40 pounds in six months. I've maintained this weight for several years, give or take the five pounds that continue to yo-yo. I used a tool called MyFitnessPal when I got started. About a year ago, my neighbor and I joined WeightWatchers to get the yo-yo weight to stop yo-yo-ing. I'm a huge fan of the recent FreeStyle enhancements to the WeightWatchers points system. Just like with financial fuel, tracking food consumption makes a huge difference.

Eating isn't only about weight management. It's primarily about health and wellness. You need the right mix of calories and nutrients to live the life camino of your dreams. Fueling your body with mostly plant-based foods, especially fruits and vegetables, organic products, and low fat proteins are keys to longevity. Avoid fried and highly processed foods. Eat more chicken and fish and go light on the red meat, saving that great steak for a special occasion. If you enjoy cooking, Google search "clean eating recipes" or "cooking light" to find mouth-watering healthy options that won't disappoint your taste buds.

Contemplate changes you can make to create healthier eating habits. What action steps will you take this week to begin making a shift?

The "a-ha!"s that showed up with reference to eating well were:

## CLEAN YOUR TANK

Gone are the days when high carb, low fat diets were the answer. Many people got fatter instead of thinner when those excess carbohydrate calories turned into belly fat. Then came the idea to never, ever skip breakfast. Next, the wisdom on healthy eating included five or six small meals a day. Despite all the effort, waistlines across America continued to expand. As a society, people became sicker instead of healthier.

The latest science shows there are tremendous health benefits from consuming calories in narrower windows of time and periodically fasting. Google "Intermittent Fasting" (IF) to learn about options that might work best for you. The IF plan that works best for me is to restrict my eating window to fewer than six to eight hours per day. That leaves 16 to 18 hours for fasting's magic to work on burning belly fat reserves. The analogy I've heard is this process is like running the gas tank in your car to near empty so that "gunk" at the bottom of the tank can be cleaned out. Apparently, your body is able to clear out damaged inefficient cells in favor of feeding and promoting growth of healthy cells through biological processes triggered by fasting. The net result of intermittent fasting is a healthier version of you.

What underpins these healthy lifestyle choices is a spirit of moderation and self-love. If I really want a slice of pizza, I have one. If dessert looks amazing, I ask myself if it's worth the calories. If so, I have a couple of bites of dessert. I only eat pasta and those beloved French baguettes on special occasions now. When I do, I savor each bite. Life is just too short to say "no" to the many food pleasures along the way.

Contemplate and research how intermittent fasting could benefit your health. What action steps will you take this week to begin making a shift?

When you tried IF, did you have any "a-ha!" moments?

## TOP OFF YOUR FLUIDS

One of the last things my dad did before a summer trip to grandma's house was top off the oil, windshield washer fluid, and anti-freeze levels in the car. This analogy of topping off fluids is especially impactful for me because topping off my fluids by drinking more water was one of the toughest health habits for me to adopt on my renewed life camino.

When I began living an IF lifestyle one of my tennis friends, also a devotee of this regimen, repeatedly reminded me to drink two large glasses of water before my morning coffee. Doing this manages hunger and flushes out toxins processed while fasting during the night before. If I had to think about this, I'd never do it. Drinking water is just not intuitive even though I understand the benefits of hydration, especially living in the desert.

I usually carry with me and do my best to finish an insulated 64-ounce version of The Coldest Water Jug. It seemed impossible to keep track of how many water bottles I'd consumed or refilled throughout the day so one big container is the perfect approach for me. Creating a system for topping off my fluids worked well because it took the thinking out of it and built the action into a routine that I'm already committed to. All I have to do is finish the jug.

Besides black coffee, I drink water and unsweetened iced tea. I've dropped sugary and artificially sweetened carbonated beverages. I feel so much better. I also drink wine on occasion, although I'm a huge advocate of January as an alcohol-free month to clean up and reset after all the holiday parties. Before, or while drinking each glass of wine, I drink a full glass of water. This is hangover prevention for those times I'm celebrating and might lose track of how much wine I'm consuming. Plus, it's a good strategy to keep topping off fluids.

Contemplate changes you could make to consume more water each day. Target drinking each day half your body weight in ounces of water. If you weigh 120 pounds, drink 60 ounces of water. What action steps will you take this week to begin making a shift?

Did you have any "a-ha!"s about topping off your fluids?

## STEPPING ONTO THE TRAIL

Now that many of the practical preparations for the journey are complete, you're ready to step onto the trail, to experience life's great adventures along the reimagined the path before you. The critical point in this next section: It's all about you. You are responsible for where your life's camino is headed. Whether you're single, married, or in a partnership walking your camino in authenticity is about recognizing and valuing your needs.

You may sometimes invite others to join you for a portion of your journey. Traveling together can be a fantastic way to experience life's adventures. Even then, you are ultimately responsible only for yourself. You are a unique individual with legitimate needs. Regardless of your relationship status, you need to learn how to get comfortable traveling solo. Only when you are happy and successful alone will you be able to share the journey with others in a healthy manner.

Traveling solo is new for me. I was in a relationship with the same man for nearly 30 years. Now I'm on my own. These past few years are the only time I've given any thought at all to the concept of traveling solo. The way I stopped talking and started learning to enjoy solo living was to take a week long vacation on my own.

Paralyzing thoughts ran through my head. Would I be safe? Would I get stuck on social media because I was uncomfortable sitting alone in a restaurant? Would I be bored with days or weeks of alone time? Would I enjoy traveling by myself? Would I ever find people with a similar wanderlust for travel so I'd have options to travel alone or with others?

My first solo trip was to Maui in the spring of 2015. I had a timeshare week I needed to use or lose which was pretty much the deciding factor in me making this trip. I tried new foods, visited out-of-the-way beaches and hiking trails, and chatted with fascinating visitors from other parts of the world. I'm grateful for this travel experience that kick-started my lessons and the exhilaration I felt exploring life on my terms and on my time schedule.

Contemplate setting aside a week or even a weekend to travel somewhere alone. Where would you go? What action steps will you take this week to begin making a shift?

The "a-ha"s you had about traveling solo were:

## GET UNCOMFORTABLE

Do you remember your first day in Driver's Education class? Perhaps you were excited but at the same time a little anxious or uncomfortable with the idea of getting behind the wheel for the first time and putting the car in gear. If you've never dealt with a temporary feeling of discomfort, your life choices today are limited. It's all about living courageously.

A good friend of mine enlightened me about the truth of "un-comfortability." Personal growth is challenging most of the time. If it were easy, none of us would spend so much energy avoiding it. "Get comfortable with feeling uncomfortable," is one of this friend's mottos. It applies to every area of my life, and probably yours, too.

Getting "comfortable with feeling uncomfortable" happened to me one afternoon not long after my divorce was final. I'm sure the self-conversation fell under the umbrella of: "What am I doing? Why am I stuck? Where am I going?"

Letting go of the belief that life needs to feel comfortable every moment opened up possibilities for my growth.

It took a lot of self-prompts (and perhaps many glasses of wine) to get the wheels in my brain turning on this important lesson. Yes, I felt stuck. Then, it occurred to me that maybe I was not taking action on my promise to start living a more authentic version of my life's camino because it wasn't comfortable. It is more comfortable to zone out by watching a mindless television show or peruse social media for hours than to wrestle with internal issues that need to be dealt with to get "unstuck."

I realized that to create the life camino of my dreams I had to figure out me. What I wanted. What I needed. What made myself "tick." I needed to deal with a cornucopia of bottled up feelings and emotional blockages. I was about to step into my truth. This new life camino required learning to get comfortable with feeling uncomfortable.

Contemplate how you might practice getting comfortable with feeling uncomfortable. Ask yourself, what is it that I avoid doing or saying because I might feel a moment of discomfort or perhaps because someone else will? What action steps will you take this week to begin making a shift?

_____

_____

_____

_____

_____

Find even one "a-ha!" realization about comfort in "uncomfortableness":

_____

_____

_____

_____

_____

## SOLO PREP

The lessons I learned while figuring out how to navigate life's journey solo apply to everyone regardless of relationship status. For some people, diving straight into a solo experience and seeing what happens will work best. For others, dipping in toes as a first step will help acclimate to this new body of water.

To practice, I took on a series of self-induced solo challenges. Solo tasks in the first self-challenge were to: 1) sit at a local bar and have a drink, 2) go to a movie, and 3) eat dinner at a table (not at the bar) in a restaurant. I kept my cell phone inaccessible for the duration of these activities, I felt free to chat with anyone, and I was open for something new to discover.

Going to a movie. Check. This was an easy, early win for me. It's dark in a movie theater so I didn't think about anything but engaging in the movie plot. Sitting at a restaurant by myself, without props to distract me was a lot more difficult. I felt a bit like I imagine an addict might feel, fidgeting in my chair, looking around wondering what to do with my hands with no social media to tend to.

The second set of self-challenges involved immersing myself in nature. Nature is noticeably more breathtaking when explored solo. I set a time to: 1) find a nearby hiking trail and head out for an hour or more, 2) head to the park with a book or journal to get lost in words, and 3) find a local farmer's market and linger, absorbing the vibrant colors and aromas of its fresh fruits and vegetables.

These types of activities turned out to be right up my alley because they engaged all my senses. I brought my trusty iPhone, took photos, sampled fruits, and breathed in the fresh air. This set of challenges reignited my passion for the great outdoors. I'd been sitting inside at a computer and in boardroom meetings far too long.

The last set of self-challenges that helped me feel comfortable doing pretty much anything solo involved: 1) driving an hour or two to a quaint nearby town for an afternoon of wandering the streets window shopping, 2) taking an afternoon class in one of my areas of interest, and 3) volunteering at a local soup kitchen and food bank.

By the time I'd made it to the third set of challenges, I knew I had going solo nailed. I was surprised and delighted to find interesting experiences everywhere, just a stone's throw from my front door. While I love traveling to the far corners of the globe, that's not practical from either a time or monetary resource management standpoint on a daily basis. Yet within my grasp every day or weekend were magical experiences previously off my radar screen.

Come up with your own self-challenge list. The only crucial selection criterion is that doing the activity alone must in some way push you out of your comfort zone. I love massages and pedicures as much or more than most people. These don't count as trial runs to practice flying solo because they're more or less solo activities by definition. Push yourself! Live the motto "get comfortable with feeling uncomfortable."

By the time you accomplish half a dozen solo activities you'll realize as I did that you don't need the crutch of another person to fully enjoy the moment. Once you feel comfortable experiencing your life's camino alone, you can be sure that when you do invite passengers along to share the ride, it's for the right reasons.

Contemplate ideas that will get you outside your comfort zone on your own. What action steps will you take this week to begin making a shift?

Perhaps you'll write a list of before-and-after "a-ha!"s when you experiment by planning to and then going out of your comfort zone:

## PICK UPS AND DROP OFFS

Once you're comfortable as a soloist, consider whether you're interested in inviting others to share small portions of your life's camino. It could be a friend who joins you for a short trip. Perhaps a child or grandchild could accompany you on a hike, or to see a play or concert.

There are longer journeys, too, but not always for the rest of your lifetime. Maybe you've chosen to remain single and adopt, foster, or volunteer with children. Perhaps being a significant influence in the life of grandchildren will be the way you "pick up and drop off" companionship. Having a partner with whom to share a close, intimate relationship may involve the "pick up and drop off" of dating and not living together.

Whatever the scenario, you are always responsible for your life journey's direction. Self-accountability is the essence of living your most authentic life camino. You are not a victim. Do not give up personal power by buying into that belief. No matter what has happened in your life find the lesson, learn from it, and move on.

When I learned to stop blaming life itself for being unfair, my boss at work for not making the right call, and the accident in front of me for making me late for an appointment, a richer life camino began unfolding for me. It's empowering to take responsibility for what's mine. It gives me the power to make a choice and create a different outcome. Life events happen for me so that I can experience life's magic and learn important lessons. Life doesn't happen to me. When the going gets tough, I ask myself, "Why is this happening <u>for</u> me?"

A single "a-ha!" moment that turned into one of my life's principles became a question I now ask myself in many situations: "Which part of this belongs to me?" Here's a real-life situation to illustrate: I wake up late, the kids aren't cooperating, my spouse is traveling for work and I leave later than expected to drop off the kids at school. I need to make it to an important early morning meeting at work. Murphy's Law (everything that can go wrong will go wrong) kicks in, and I'm annoyed to be walking in late for the meeting. My boss in a far-away time zone is ticked off and lets me know it. Like me, how many times do you mentally blame the alarm clock, the kids, your spouse, the accident along the roadway, and even your boss for why you are late or feel badly?

In those types of too-close-to-home scenarios, I learned to ask, "What do I own here? What could I have done differently?" The message: only this part of the situation belongs to you. Maybe you own 80 percent while 20 percent belongs to others. Some percentage always belongs to you. Take the percentage that belongs to you. Own it. Tell yourself it's OK. Commit to making different choices next time. Let the rest go. Mentally and emotionally send the energy of the situation that isn't yours away from your space.

Contemplate a recent situation where you allowed yourself to feel like a victim. Reframe this and ask yourself, "Why did this situation happen for me? What part do I own?" What action steps will you take this week to begin making a shift?

What have you "owned" that gave you an "a-ha!" moment as a victor, not a victim?

## MERGE TRAILS

Merging, and safely sharing the road with others, is an important life concept that dovetails with going with the flow, showing respect, and appreciating the element of timing.

As a person once very "in like" with the idea of certainty, I found going with the flow was easier to talk about than put into practice. It's an intuitive lesson. Everything in life has its pace and timing. Vegetable seeds are planted in the spring, grow through the summer, and are harvested in the fall. In the winter, the ground rests. Harvesting corn when it isn't ready wastes everybody's time.

The same is true with life's camino. You are not the only person on the pathway. There are others going different places at different speeds. You need to merge into traffic along the camino in a way that claims your unique space on the path while respecting what's happening around you.

This means accepting and embracing journeys that are different from your own — not shoving people out of the way, nor attempting to force them into traveling in your lane, at your speed, and toward your destination.

This can be an especially difficult lesson to learn when applied to one's children. Yes, it's your responsibility to raise them with good values, provide a safe and secure home, give them a solid education, and get them prepared for life as independent adults. Having the wisdom to step back and recognize that their life lessons may be very different from yours is an important part of your life's camino. You have the right to live life on your terms because you give space to those around you to live life on their terms. It's about respect.

Parents often have difficulty letting children go live their dreams. Sometimes, parents are desperate to see children live a version of perfect life, to avoid the mistakes where tough lessons are learned. This desperation robs children of the lessons that are part of the magic of life itself. You are the perfectly imperfect person you are today because of decisions, and perhaps mistakes, made along the way. Some of these situations worked out far better than you'd imagined and other decisions didn't work out as well as you'd hoped. You learned. You grew. You became the interesting, flawed, somewhat self-aware person you are today. Aren't your favorite book or movie characters the quirky ones who have lovable "flaws?" They aren't perfect. They fall, they get up, and they keep on trying.

Merging well is also about timing. While you're going with the flow and respecting others on the road, it's also important to keep moving at the speed and in the direction you need to go. It's an important lesson to understand the art of not getting stuck behind slower drivers or boxed in by others wanting to change lanes or exit the roadway. Timing is about staying true to your needs, living your life's camino on your terms, and being aware of others sharing the road with you. Some of these travelers will journey along side you for quite a distance. You'll enjoy many experiences together. Others may quickly pass and exit at the next crossroads for an entirely different destination. When you learn to share the road successfully, you know you are on the way to living an inspired life camino.

Contemplate how you might practice allowing others to travel their journey and learn life lessons different from yours without judgment. What action steps will you take this week to begin making a shift?

"Ah-ha!"s related to observing others without judgment were:

Camino: Reimagining the Path

## FILTERS

Everyone makes hundreds of decisions in a day, some without a conscious thought, simply based on how their filters are set. You tune in to information that's important to you because part of your brain, known as the Reticular Activating System (RAS), constantly filters through billions of bits of data and miraculously gives you access to the information you need, when you need it.

Did you ever have the experience of being in a new place and not noticing a gas station, FedEx store, or Starbucks for miles? When you think of a need for gasoline or coffee, these locations seem to pop up on every corner. Do you know how when you're sound asleep you'll wake up the second you hear your baby cry? These are examples of your RAS at work.

Filters are important. You couldn't function without them. How do you come by these filters? Your filters are as unique as your fingerprints. They're created and reinforced by your beliefs, your childhood programming, and your life experiences. Filters are necessary for making decisions. Filters go awry and get in the way of your life's camino when you use your decision-making skills to judge others.

There's a fantastic coloring journal written by an author friend of mine, ShaRon Rea called *No Judgment. Just Love.* ShaRon reminds you to allow your life, and the lives of others you meet on the journey to "just be," especially those who may think or feel differently than you do, or those you simply don't understand. Her messages of kindness and unconditional love, to go with the flow and stop judging, fit perfectly with this life transformation journey that is common to everyone.

An interesting twist about her book is that even though 90 percent of the population is right handed, the 10 percent who are left-handed were considered, and they have their own version of *No Judgment. Just Love.* What a great opportunity to reinforce the "no judgment" message by offering two versions. The books are intended to help children develop "no judgment" filters, but honestly, it's fun for adults to channel their inner child and use this coloring journal to reflect on their own filters as well.

Contemplate where your life filters might benefit from an adjustment or two. Where can you put in practice today the idea of "No Judgment. Just Love?" What action steps will you take this week to begin making a shift?

The shift into "No Judgment. Just Love." "a-ha!"s were:

## TUNE YOUR RADIO

Traveling in peace and quiet is usually my preference. The path mesmerizes me. I can drift into imaging the possibilities of another exotic locale I might visit. Or, ruminate over a life lesson I'm "this close" to understanding. Sometimes I enjoy listening to the radio. There are many stations from which I can choose; news, sports, talk radio, advice shows, and music stations. Each of these stations runs on its' own frequency. When looking for a specific channel, I know the frequency, the call numbers I need to tune into on the radio dial.

Just like radio stations, each person has a channel or frequency to broadcast their voice with its unique insights and messages. There are some stations – people – you might prefer not to listen to. You have the choice not to tune in to those channels. These channels have as much of a right to exist and share their message as you do. I've learned that lesson of respect. Living life on my terms means everyone else gets to live life on their terms, as well.

This insight about radio channels helped me learn an important skill that I first applied in challenging work environments. Later, I recognized how helpful this mental framework is for me in talking about difficult emotional topics. Perhaps this technique will help you. I call it, "Own the Room."

Imagine the space you are in right now as a room. Set your intention to tune in and own the frequency that belongs to your soul alone. The way I do it is to concentrate first on feeling my feet firmly planted on the ground. I get grounded. Next, I imagine rays or arrows from my heart going toward each of the upper four corners of the space. Last, I set an intention to share my truth always, and with compassion. I remind myself that no one else has the power or responsibility to share this message from my unique perspective. Then I say what I need to say. Sometimes it's difficult. Each time I find the courage to do this, I am the most authentic unstoppable version of myself.

Contemplate how you might practice "Owning the Room" or showing respect for a radio station (person) you don't naturally prefer. What action steps will you take this week to begin making a shift?

Your "a-ha!"s on attention to frequency are important — what are they?

## CROWN JEWELS

One of my life's great joys is the feeling of freedom I get when the sun is shining bright and the wind is whipping through my hair as I drive my convertible with the windows open and the top down. I've thought about the inner conflict created by the times I operated my vehicle to suit someone else's preferences. Perhaps they thought I went too fast or too slow, it was too warm or too cold, or they didn't enjoy the wind blowing through their hair. Whichever the scenario, I settled. Settling is not the same as compromising. Settling is giving up your dream or forgoing your needs to try to make someone else happy. Compromising is agreeing to a middle ground that meets the needs of both individuals traveling together on the journey.

I realized I'd been settling too often. It was never the other person's fault. Most of the time they never asked me to settle I just assumed what they wanted and adjusted my course. I wasn't courageous or aware enough to articulate my needs or desires; I may not have even been in touch with them.

One of the steps along my life transformation process allowed me to learn the "crown jewels" lesson. It illustrates the concept of settling. Crown jewels are a monarchy's accessories that are passed from one generation to the next. There are crowns, scepters, orbs, swords, rings, and other items included in the collection of crown jewels. I like the visual of the crown itself, but any of these items creates the same analogy.

Imagine you are wearing your unique crown, and it's filled with precious gemstones that represent your inner beauty, talents, hopes, and dreams. The crown and its jewels brilliantly reflect the day's sunlight with a rainbow of vibrant colors. This is you "on fire" for your life's camino.

Now imagine that as you meet people along the way you take jewels out from your crown or you hide it altogether to make others feel more comfortable. This is not living your authentic life camino. Once I thought about and understood this powerful analogy, I mentally drew a line in the sand and made the choice to stop taking jewels out of my crown. I decided to stop settling for people and situations that make me shine less bright than I was made to shine.

Contemplate recent situations where you settled or took jewels out of your crown to make someone else feel more comfortable. What action steps will you take this week to begin making a shift?

Your "a-ha!"s about your "crown jewels" are:

## TRAVEL BINGO

When we drove the two hours from our small hometown along the Mississippi river in Minnesota to grandma's house in central Wisconsin, my brother and I played travel bingo. This of course was played the "old school" way, eons before cellphones and handheld gaming devices were invented.

For those of you unfamiliar with travel bingo, it's similar to regular bingo. Each player receives a 5 x 5 grid with the same 25 road trip-related items illustrated square-by-square. The first person to spot all the items a row or column shouts "Bingo!" and is declared the winner. Items on the card include things like a speed limit sign, purple wildflower, barn, police car, etc. I'm certain we used hand drawn grids prepared by our mom, but you can print free ones at www.travelchannel.com.

Travel bingo taught me a few important lessons at a young age. One was how to be competitive without being mean-spirited toward to my younger brother. This made the drive more enjoyable for everyone. The other lesson is that I paid attention, and learned to "notice what I notice."

As an adult, I see the concept of "notice what you notice" as a call to search for the meaning or lesson in what's happening around me. For example, in a situation where someone annoys me, instead of reacting, or more likely over-reacting, I ask myself to "notice" what's really happening. Usually I come away with an insight I would have otherwise missed. Maybe it's that I'm feeling annoyed because I'm tired and my annoyance has nothing to do with the other person's behavior. Maybe it was the third time today this person pushed my buttons. After the "notice," I'll ask if there's something going on with them that they want to talk about. Maybe I'll see that I'm personalizing something that truly has nothing to do with me and I'm more able to just let it go.

Since everyone is a traveler on life's camino, let's play the adult version of travel bingo and focus on "noticing what we notice".

Contemplate how you might practice "noticing what you notice." What important lessons you learned in grade school might travel bingo bring up for you? What action steps will you take this week to begin making a shift?

Fill this space with "a-ha!"s that relate to the idea that "you notice what you notice."

## SIGN LANGUAGE

Wouldn't it be great if there were signs along the way to guide your life? These signs would alert you to changing conditions. Life signs are everywhere just as traffic signs are, and it is up to you to notice them.

These thoughts tumbled around my brain for some time before answers began to emerge. Now, I'm certain that life signs are available to be seen and meant for you and me — they're everywhere, all the time. Set an intention to notice the signs to activate your RAS and begin seeing them. This is known as synchronicity. Understanding the signs is simply another language to learn to successfully navigate your life's camino.

As with all languages, with practice you will become more fluent. With some degree of sign reading fluency in hand, I smiled when a "Speed Bump" sign appeared. That sign was located in a place I'd walked by at least a dozen times during the month I'd been nestled in the cozy Maui rental, while on sabbatical to recharge and re-center my life. Most of the time, I left my car parked in its designated spot in the parking lot. I opted to walk everywhere I could. I had the time. Aside from the errant hurricane, Maui is a tropical paradise, much of which is perfect for exploring on foot. It's funny I'd never noticed the "Speed Bump" sign or understood its message earlier in the month. Signs are like that. If the timing of the message isn't right, the RAS filters out the information and you don't notice it. Even so, the sign is still there waiting patiently.

    Like your first time behind the wheel of a car, perhaps you just need some curiosity and a bit of guidance to notice life signs — synchronicities — and learn how to interpret them. What if help is available at every turn and you're filtering it out? Maybe you're just not paying attention. Maybe you choose to believe there are no signs and so your subconscious filters them out. Maybe you believe you must navigate this life on your own and it simply never occurs to you to ask for help. I re-activated my RAS, honed my skills, and learned to interpret the signs that were important for my life's camino. So can you.

Contemplate for a moment how to dial up the sign language on your life's camino. What action steps will you take this week to begin making a shift?

Every synchronicity is an "a-ha!" moment. Write some that you've experienced.

## NAVIGATION

I don't know where I first came across the idea of the Global Positioning System. It's been around for a while. It's such a great metaphor and life lesson it needs to be included in this camino guide.

The truth is, you are going to make some wrong turns along your life's camino. It's inevitable. Not to worry. There are many routes that will get you to your destination. Think about it. You dial into Google Maps the address of the new restaurant you have reservations at for dinner. Two or three options are presented, each with different estimated arrival times. Some routes take the interstate while others take you only on local roads. You choose the route that suits you based on your criteria and preferences. Once you're on the way, you sometimes make a wrong turn. Other times you intentionally take a different road because of unfavorable traffic conditions ahead. The GPS continuously re-routes so you get to your desired destination as efficiently as possible.

There are two critical actions required on your part. The GPS takes care of the rest.

First, decide where you want to go. You set the vision for your life's camino. Your job is to dream big and feel the vision come alive. The GPS needs to be given a destination. Those instances when you've felt lost or unsure of where you were going may have been times you've paused to rest and absorb a lesson. You haven't programmed a destination so the GPS is silent. Vision is closely linked with purpose. The vision of where I want to go or what I want to experience lines up with why I am living on this planet at this particular time. What is my purpose? This is a question worth pondering. I'm a seeker of personal growth. I fill up with energy when I begin to understand important life lessons that help me grow. My purpose has everything to do with helping others learn and grow. When your purpose is clear and it's used to touch the lives of others in a positive way, all humanity evolves and becomes a better version of its own mass consciousness.

Second, you need to move. It's not enough to understand your purpose and have a vision. You need to take action. Because the GPS is able to see the big picture, it can deftly re-route your journey as you run into roadblocks or adjust course. If you remain stationary, the GPS (even if it is programmed) will not be able to help. Go step-by-step. Inches at first; then feet, yards, meters, kilometers, miles.

That's how the camino of life is made.

This is not to say you need to have the details of "how" you are to get somewhere completely mapped out. You'd never take action if you needed to know every step along a winding path filled with unexpected adventures. That's why the GPS is available to manage the overall picture. I've talked myself out of taking action many times by "not being ready," or "not being sure exactly where this is going." Now I see that it wasn't my job to be ready, or to see where I was going. It's not your job, either. You know everything you need to know to take action now. What you need to know later will become clear as you move along the path. Whatever feels right is the correct next step. Don't overthink it. The quote below is a great reminder of this principle.

*Caminante no hay camino se hace camino al andar.*

Translation:

*Traveler, there is no road; you make your own path*
*as you walk.*

*~ Antonio Machado*

Contemplate where along your life's camino creating a heartfelt vision or taking some small steps would kick your GPS into gear. What action steps will you take this week to begin making a shift?

The GPS may be programmed or not — what are your "a-ha!"s?

## CROSSROADS

Think about crossroads. Go beyond those times when you're waiting at a four-way stop sign and a decision needs to be made. You're at a crossroads when the needs of others are pulling you in multiple directions, and there is an overall lack of clarity about your vision. The skill to dealing with being at this kind of a crossroad is called "Managing the Middle."

Consciously or not, you invite into your life various people and situations that require decisions. All have roles of varying degrees of importance in the multi-act theatre performance that is your life. Most people and situations show up as part of your life story's plotline for a couple of reasons. One is to enable the experience of emotion, whether fun, drama, fear, sympathy, sadness, bliss, or any other of the countless possibilities. Another reason they are here is to help you learn lessons you need to grow into a better version of yourself. Many times these people reside in the spaces you've invited them into to make both of you feel comfortable and in control.

What about the less comfortable times, times that challenge or frustrate you? Perhaps the people haven't answered your questions or met your needs, or, you're in a situation where you can't make up your mind. These are the spots along life's journey where you are stuck waiting at a crossroads.

I'm sure there are people in your life with whom you would really like to engage at a deeper level. They just can't seem to make up their mind about what they want, or they're so busy they don't have time to spend with you. This could be a family member with whom you've had some struggles or a good friend who's busy prioritizing a job or kids ahead of you. This could be someone you would like to develop a romantic relationship with. This theme has many scenarios.

Look at other situations in life that follow that same pattern. You want to get in shape but you just are not able. You'd like a more fulfilling job but you stay in your current one. You think maybe you should remodel, sell, rent a new place, or ... maybe not do anything at all with your living space. You'd like to live your new and improved life's camino but you just don't have the time or money to get started. Whether you think it's "them" creating the issue or you, it's you. You are always in control of making the best decision for you. Own your power and don't let victim thinking nudge its way onto your life's camino.

This lesson challenged me to learn that allowing people and situations to live in the middle was holding me back from living the life camino of my dreams. I spent too much time waiting for other people, waiting for the perfect time to do something, or avoiding making a tough decision — I was "Managing the Middle." What are any of us waiting for? Why are you waiting?

This is not a call to cut loose everyone and everything you're waiting on. Sometimes allowing the middle to exist for a time is beneficial for an important lesson to sink in, or to rest and reflect before the next act of your life story unfolds.

The ultimate goal is to navigate life out of the stuck middle and onto the fun fringes of growth and living life on your terms. What exactly do you need to do? Accept that decision-making is not always comfortable, put on your "big-girl" or "big-boy" pants, and make a call.

Keep in mind that a non-decision by you or others is in fact a type of "no." Stop wasting time and energy trying to convince yourself or others to change a middle ground, non-answer "no" to a "yes." Accept the soft "no" by being gentle, and intentionally moving these people and situations out of your everyday physical and emotional space. Invest your precious time and energy where it counts by taking the steps to your reimagined life.

Contemplate situations where you continue to stay stuck "Managing the Middle" in ways that no longer serve you. What action steps will you take this week to begin making a shift?

Go beyond "Managing the Middle" to find some "a-ha!"s:

## ASK FOR HELP

The first thing I do when I arrive in a foreign country is head to the local tourism office. It's the fastest and easiest way to get the lay of the land and to understand the highlights and hidden gems of that location. I talk to the locals I meet at the coffee shop or in the hotel's reception area, in the basics of their language if possible, to find out where the restaurants are they like or what they think are the most enticing aspects of their town. I put myself in extrovert mode and ask for help from the locals, the experts.

Why is asking for help so difficult? Maybe it's pride; you might think you'd be better off figuring out a situation on your own. Maybe you don't want to be bothersome. Perhaps you learned as a child to complete homework or paper routes with no help and that patterned a self-reliant streak. When you don't seek and use information that's readily available, you miss important insights that can enhance your life's camino.

In addition to the help you can tap into at your travel destinations, there's help all around you when you tap into your intuition, or inner voice, or gut feelings. These three phrases are all interconnected elements of the same concept. Which term is more familiar to you?

For me, it's intuition. My intuition re-emerged loud and clear once I reconnected my head and my heart. Some of you may scratch your head at the idea of having a disconnected heart and head. The way I experience it, it's a situation where thinking and feeling are compartmentalized instead of working together as they were designed.

There are many ways to connect your head and your heart. Search the Internet for ideas that speak to you.

The way I practice reconnecting my head and heart is by having mental conversations with my inner child. I call her Lizzie, my nickname. I imagine her as my inner child as opposed to my inner self. This is brings to the surface pure, innocent child-like wisdom that adults forget. The inner child image also reminds me of the courageous, fun, playful, not-so-serious side of me that can get lost in adult life.

When I wake up in the morning, I feel like I need to reconnect with myself, so I typically stretch and set my intentions for the day. Often I have a mental conversation with Lizzie before I get out of bed. I ask her how she feels and what she wants. I ask for her help with difficult situations I need to manage that day. I thank her for always being there for me and with me along this exciting life camino. I also ask to be reminded of her presence with visible signs throughout the day.

Feathers are important reminders that seem to float my way after I've understood important concepts or messages. I also deliberately place objects in my line of sight to remind me of the help that's always available to me. Some especially meaningful objects are a carved open palm the size of a quarter from a trip to Peru, a shell from the Camino de Santiago, sunflowers, lit candles, and a rustic bead bracelet.

Contemplate things you could do to access your intuition more easily. What visible symbols might you wish to place nearby to remind you help is always available? What action steps will you take this week to begin making a shift?

Write some "a-ha!"s that come from yourself as well as your inner child:

## SLOW YOUR ROLL

I've had my share of speeding tickets. Considering the amount of time I've spent driving over the speed limit, I probably should have been gifted more of them. I'm a safe driver. I just like driving fast, walking fast, and getting where I'm going fast.

Besides the obvious safety concerns associated with speed and the cost of unplanned tickets or accidents, there's another insight I've gleaned from this metaphor. At times, I need to slow my roll, to slow down, and be more present. It seems to me that people generally choose to live in the past or the future. Past-living people reminisce about how great high school was or how terrible their family dynamics were. Future-directed people focus on planning the next great adventure and trying to get to the next event as quickly as possible.

To live your life's camino with authenticity, put your focus on the present moment. For me, this means slowing down and noticing the little things that bring me joy. I want to fully enjoy the moments while drinking a glass of wine with a friend or the experience of visiting an off-the-beaten-path café or shop. You step into the present when you put down your cellphone. My number one life principle, and one I'd highly recommend you adopt, is that the cellphone stays off and in my purse when I'm with friends. People are "un-present" when sitting at a restaurant table with friends or family members while posting to Instagram and checking Facebook.

Learning how to overcome boredom should be done during childhood — but it's never too late. The accessibility of electronic information, communication, gaming, and learning erases one's ability to have "nothing to do." Eons ago when I was growing up, my friends, my brother and I had plenty of time on our hands. We didn't have access to instant gratification and constant stimulation. When children and even adults create space to just be and even be bored, they have to be creative in thinking and with problem solving. They see the little things and thus experience more magical moments that life offers in the natural environment, and away from the screens.

Contemplate whether you more often look in the rearview mirror or imagine the "what's next." What action steps will you take this week to begin making a shift to live more in the present?

Write some "a-ha!"s in this present moment of time:

## STOP LITTERING

Walking through Honokowai, a small town along Maui's western coast, the strangest sign found its way to me with a life message: "No Dumping, Drains to Ocean." I reflected on where my life was a few short years ago when the world I had created was gearing up for a seismic, scary shift.

I'd married at age 28, after graduating from college, being established in a career I loved, and having dated my husband-to-be for five years. I was mature, and sure I knew where my life was going. I had it all mapped out.

Then, 25 years, two grown kids and a dog later, I knew so much more. My unsettled gut told me something was about to change — something needed to change. My perfectly groomed and designed life unraveled. I found myself telling tales of woe and blaming of others or life itself on anyone who would listen. I was dumping personal toxic waste. These stories were dumped and re-dumped over and over again. Then, just when I needed it most, a good friend re-appeared to pull me up to saner ground where I could see more clearly, learn some important lessons, stop dumping toxicity, and move forward.

Dumping is never healthy. It's about getting rid of thoughts or things with the energy of reckless abandon. Dump it down the drain or into a landfill. You just want to get all the bad energy away from you, and now. There are a number of problems with this.

First, dumping your trash and running means you are avoiding the lessons you are meant to learn. Dumping comes from a place of victimhood. You are not living as your most powerful self or being accountable for your choices and actions. Avoiding it means repeating it. The only way is through. There truly is no around. I've tried it. Trust me on this wisdom.

Second, dumping drains your drama, chaos, and angst to the "ocean" and pollutes your friends' lives and the environment. Owning your story, and creating healthy boundaries so you can share your truth without contaminating the lives of others is what puts you on the higher ground.

Beyond owning your stuff and dealing with it, consider the impact you have on the environment and others who are traveling life's road alongside you. Their path is different from your path. In addition to curtailing the dumping, be mindful of not littering. Littering is not as extreme as dumping but it has a negative environmental effect. A careless hurtful comment tossed on the path of another can pollute their environment just like a used tissue rolling around on the ground pollutes the landscape. In living life on your terms, it's important to care for trash in a responsible manner and respect the journey of others who are traveling nearby.

Contemplate times when you may have been guilty of metaphorical dumping or littering recently. What action steps will you take this week to begin making a shift?

Your "a-ha!" stories regarding dumping and littering emotions are:

# STOPPING ALONG THE WAY

Stops are necessary for all travelers on life's camino. Your job is to generally prepare for your life's camino and then to enjoy the ride without knowing details about all the stops you'll make. This is what keeps the journey interesting. It's not about the destination — it's about the lessons you learn. The stops along the way are meant to be unexpected, unknowable, and unlimited in their potential. Stops give you the rest you need to check your perspective.

To find inspiration for potential stops on my life's camino, I created a folder titled: Imagine the Possibilities. I tore out pictures and quotes from magazines that spoke to me. I thought about my three to five priorities that spark joy and looked for online pictures and phrases that best illustrated them. It was a joy-filled, divergent, creative exercise wandering through possibilities of the experiences I might enjoy to the places I might visit one day. There were pictures of healthy active living, joyful relationships with friends and family, candles, massages, and zen-like moments, plus travel destinations from national parks to islands in the Mediterranean. It was energizing! I dreamed big. Nothing was off limits.

I then found a digital version of everything I'd collected on paper and organized the content into folders on my computer. I was tempted to print everything and create a large envelope filled with ideas so I could more easily see, feel, and touch them, but the tidy person in me encouraged me to go the digital route. Every January, I revisit this process. I toss out the ideas that no longer fit, put the ones I've accomplished in another folder, and add new pictures and quotes to the mix.

The "a-ha!" moments that arrive after this exercise is done are worth every bit of time you invested. For example, instead of a folder, a friend created a vision board (pictures only), and filled out a two-page sheet of "instructions" for herself in the areas of: career, relationships, finances, and health/self-care. One of her pictures depicted an uncluttered office environment that she felt represented a more positive way to operate her business. Within weeks, she'd re-organized her workspace (a much easier task than she'd expected) and had attracted contracts for projects ideal in scope and scale for her talents, making her feel so much better about managing time spent on work and in leisure.

Contemplate and then create your version of an Imagine the Possibilities folder. What action steps will you take this week to begin making a shift?

Once your folder is done, you'll have "a-ha!"s for sure. Record them here:

## TAKE A BREAK: GO LOCAL

Life camino transformation provides an opportunity to explore your local environment. Going local is great way to take small steps in expanding your horizons and experiencing life on your terms sooner versus later. So, take a break! Discover nearby activities that elevate your spirit and make your heart sing. I love exploring the world – even when it's a part of the world that's right around the corner. Make a list of what "going local" means to you. Immerse yourself in experiences in areas you're passionate about.

Pull out your Imagine the Possibilities folder, and spend some time researching local options for fun that intrigue you. It might help you get started to try building on some of the ideas from clippings in your folder. If one of your interests is art, search for "art festivals," "art exhibitions," "art museums," "outdoor art," "local art," or, "free art." In each search, include the name of your town or city of residence.

Sign up for email newsletters from local newspapers and organizations with a focus on priority interest areas. Check out events they are promoting for the upcoming month or weekend. Many of these events are free. You'll be surprised by all of the artists, markets, and events available close to home. One time I Google searched "weekend activities" and found a tattoo festival complete with local street artists, food trucks, and music. Way off the grid of my typical Saturday, yet this find created the opportunity for a fun and unexpected experience.

Look at a map to find small towns less than an hour or two away from home that you could visit in a day. TripAdvisor lists popular activities. In Arizona, I visited nearby Jerome and learned that the world's largest kaleidoscope store is located in Jerome. The beautiful designs in that quirky shop were mesmerizing. I enjoyed a perfect, spontaneous afternoon exploring and came home with great memories and photos.

More recently, I found myself at a Native American restaurant for lunch on a Sunday afternoon in Ajo, Arizona. In addition to viewing some fantastic street art in nearby Artist's Alley, I found beautifully hand painted eggshells filled with confetti called cascarones and learned about the tradition of using them as part of a typical Easter celebration. Unexpected finds create unexpected joy-filled moments.

In every city and town, there are local attractions that tourists deliberately come from out of town to visit. The year-round residents typically don't take the time to experience them. Local discovery and immersion is the easiest way to experience the camino of your dreams, particularly early in the process while you're saving for your big-ticket adventures.

Contemplate and conceive of some specific local activities you feel drawn to. What action steps will you take this week to begin making a shift?

_____
_____
_____



When you have an "a-ha!" moment at a local attraction, record it here:

_____
_____
_____
_____

## MOTHER NATURE

At the top of my list of camino stops is anything and everything involving exploration of the great outdoors. Nature is accessible to all. It's likely you'll find a local park, nature area, or public open land a short distance from your home. Also likely nearby is a public bike trail or a hiking trail through the woods or desert.

Within a few hours' drive, bus, or train ride of your home, there are state parks and national parks with gorgeous views filled with natural beauty. These parks make a great day trip solo or with family and friends. If you're going to get your national park mojo into full swing, invest in an annual pass (www.nps.gov). For $80 per year, you and your family are provided with unlimited access to all of the national parks in the United States. If you're 62 and over, there's a one-time $80 fee for a senior national parks pass with no expiration date. For anyone living in the central part of the United States, the Great Smoky Mountains National Park is always free to enter. I spent five days exploring that park recently but wanted to stay at least a month. It's filled with trails, scenic hikes to waterfalls, wildlife, stunning vistas, and parts of the Appalachian Trail.

I'm a fan of stops along the way involving nature because they take me off the grid. If you plan visit times well, you'll avoid crowds. Find a sense of peace, and a lot of wonder when you are outdoors. Hear birds sing, feel the comforting embrace of the forest while walking along a trail, or stop and listen to the sounds of small waters flowing in a brook. It's the best place I know to do some deep breathing. There are no distractions. When you bring friends, ask them to stop with you at times along the path. Remind each other to soak it all in. These visits to places of natural beauty offer great opportunities for unique photographs; lush shades of green moss carpeting the tree bark or an unexpected close up of a giant mushroom on the forest floor. Nature provides the opportunity to clear your mind and recharge your battery.

I explore a trail or visit a new park about once a month. Living in Arizona, the weather almost always cooperates. For those living in other states or countries with more varied seasonal conditions, you'll find just as many opportunities for adventures in all kinds of weather. To experience the same park blanketed in wintertime snow versus filled with wildflowers in the spring expands your perspective.

What's the closest state park or national park you could visit in the next four weeks for a day or a weekend? Get it on your calendar. Day trips are perfect but when possible, stay overnight in or near the park. Check out options from quaint cabins with running water and showers to lodges that are located within or just outside most national parks. Check the National Parks website (www.nps.gov) to search for accommodations. Set up camp, or find a nearby hotel — just spend some time at night beneath the billions of stars you can see when there's no light pollution.

Contemplate the possibilities Mother Nature offers and brainstorm some specific options to visit. What action steps will you take this week to begin making a shift?

Take your "natural high" to an "a-ha!" moment and write it here:

## BUTTERFLIES

Butterflies are part of Mother Nature's domain. In addition to their mesmerizing beauty, they're an important life transformation metaphor. For both you and me, butterflies are visible reminders of who we are and who we are becoming.

Here's what I learned about butterflies in science class long ago. There are several stages the organism goes through on its way to becoming a butterfly. At each stage is a different goal. Eggs are laid on leaves. Once hatched, they become caterpillars. As caterpillars grow, they shed their skin when they outgrow it. Grown caterpillars enter a chrysalis and become pupae. Inside the chrysalis, a huge transformation from pupa to butterfly takes place. To gain strength to fly and thrive in its new environment, the pupa-butterfly must struggle. The butterfly has no idea about the need for the struggle or that something amazing is about to happen as it transforms into an entity beautiful beyond its wildest imagination. If you try to help the butterfly escape the chrysalis before it's ready, the butterfly will never have the strength to fly. It will die without becoming what it was meant to be. If left alone, in its final stage, the adult butterfly emerges from the chrysalis and flies into the freedom of its being.

Butterflies remind me that I had no idea what was coming next as I struggled through life decisions and found the courage to begin taking baby steps to live my life's camino in a new way. The struggles and the lessons were important stops that shaped me into the person I am today.

I see butterflies almost every day. I have several butterfly pictures in my "Imagine the Possibilities" folder. Butterflies show me that life is a process with different stages and lessons, and when struggles are present, there is a purpose for them. I need to keep working through any challenge while trusting that transformation will be worth the effort.

Contemplate how the butterfly metaphor resonates with your life and look for butterflies that cross your path. What action steps will you take this week to begin making a shift?

Think of the butterfly metaphor and write an "a-ha!" experience that's personal to you:

## THE DOORS

You're wondering about doors, right? Those who are musical might recognize The Doors as a popular band from the 1960s, featuring Jim Morrison, but the doors you should give attention are the openings to stops along your life's camino. These doors are literal doors.

This story takes me back to my first trip along the Camino de Santiago. As I walked through village after village with more cows and chickens than people, I was intrigued by many doors of bright colors in the cobblestone walls along the narrow road through town. They weren't obvious entrances to homes or yards, just doors randomly placed in walls. Some were bright blue, some a grassy green; others were shades of yellow. Each had a unique shape. They most definitely weren't like the doors I've seen in Arizona. These doors were never open nor were there people around to ask about them. If there was a door handle, it was not a prominent feature. I wondered if these were real doors that actually opened, or props on a Camino movie set.

I'd figured out by this time that pretty much everything I noticed along the Camino had a lesson for me. I let my mind wander. I remember experiencing these differently colored closed doors on the Camino with a feeling of excitement and intrigue. What was behind them? As I contemplated my recent past, I realized there had been brightly colored metaphorical doors at every turn. I noticed them with curiosity but for years didn't try to open any of them and look inside. Why? I was too afraid of the wonderful things that might be possible if I changed my life. I hung out in the safe, comfortable life space I'd created. I never seriously considered approaching the doors at that time. I thought, "What if I took the risk to change my life and regretted it?" Eventually I chose courage over fear. I opened a bright colored door in front of me that felt like the right one and stepped forward.

There are closed doors beckoning you to open them at all points along your life's camino. It's your job to notice them. Open the ones that feel right and let the doors that need to close behind do so. Seeing the doors and finding courage to open them is what began my life transformation. There will be doors on your path as you wander through daily life. Perhaps photograph them. There are all kinds of interesting doors; antique Shoji wooden doors, barn doors, rounded doors in archways, doors within doors for little people, and Dutch half doors, sliding doors, even doggie doors! Take in the door metaphor and use this visual reminder to start looking for doors that call you in new direction.

Contemplate the door metaphor and tune your radar to notice the doors that appear along your path. What action steps will you take this week to begin making a shift?

Open a door, write an "a-ha!" about what happened next:

## OCEANS

I love water. If you're into astrology even a little, you know water signs can't get enough of that H2O. Some of the clearest lessons I've learned relate to water. The ocean is one life camino stop full of lessons. It's a place of captivating beauty filled with both unpredictable riptides and calm soothing surf. Oceans represent nature at its finest. The ocean is also a fantastic metaphor.

I was relaxing on a tiny crescent of sandy beach in Hawaii one summer day, talking with a good friend about, what else, romantic relationships. "What do we want, exactly?" we mused. Is it the easy, breezy independence of being single? But independence has a lonely side. Is it the intensity of a deeply committed partnership? Partnership requires so much effort. Just dating here and there for the fun of meeting new people can be time consuming, filled with hours of pointless conversation. It really is hard to know, much less attract what you want in the area of close, intimate relationship with another human being. With wine's assistance, the conversation shifted to discussing different types of watery environments and how they might be like different types of relationships.

At most community swimming pools, there's a shallow end and a deep end. Generally one can play in the shallow end without restrictions and enjoy the water's shallowness. It's fun and little is required in terms of attention or skill. To enter the waters of the deep end requires some level of proficiency with swimming. There's more to experience in the deep end (by doing cannonballs off the diving board to swimming laps) but there's also more that can go wrong when your feet can no longer touch bottom. At least there's the side of the pool to grab onto when you're in over your head.

As great as pools are, for some there's the unexplainable allure of the ocean, that vastness as far as the eye can see, the variety of its rough waves and calm waters, its unknown depths.

I asked my friend, "Which watery environment are you envisioning for your next romance? Is it the shallow end, the deep end, or the ocean?"

We surmised that any of these places were interesting visits. We'd appreciated the joyful simplicity of the shallow end. We'd flailed around in the deep end of the pool. And, we'd each been with partners who'd preferred the shallow end, or the deeps, when we'd wanted the opposite. We'd stood along the seashore contemplating what's possible with another human being and even waded into the water a few feet. We discussed our few friends who'd held hands and ran joyfully into the ocean with another brave soul and figured out how to navigate the ocean's water as a couple.

Beyond its use as a metaphor to clarify thinking about the type of intimate relationship I might desire, the ocean challenges me to think about where I'm going, what I want, and what's possible on my life's camino ... but only when I move away from the certainty of the shore, the pool's edge, or the shallow end. Here's a quote from a book titled *P.S. I Love You* by H. Jackson Brown Jr. that sums it up very well:

> *Twenty years from now you will be more disappointed by the things that you didn't do than by the ones you did do. So throw off the bowlines. Sail away from the safe harbor. Catch the trade winds in your sails. Explore. Dream. Discover.*

Contemplate some of your life choices with respect to intimate relationships. Have you made a conscious choice about playing in the shallow end, the deep end, or the ocean? What action steps will you take this week to begin making a shift?

Everyone has an "a-ha!" or two about close, intimate relationships ... what are a few of yours?

## FOOD STOPS

Some of the best stops along my life's camino involved checking out the broad array of food and wine options available to me. Planning ahead for a variety of food experiences is crucial for both your budget and your waistline. The great news is with some simple forethought you can have it all. Here are eight tips I discovered that are cost-effective and delight my inner foodie while I'm away from home on an extended trip.

1. Home Base Eating and Drinking. Plan to cook most meals at your home base by seeking out and testing new recipes that provide an experience of the local foods and flavors. Even if you don't typically like to cook, the act of preparing a meal at your destination is both a budget stretching opportunity and a creative experience.

2. Spice It Up. If you are traveling by car, train, bus, or other non-TSA checked carrier, figure out what spices you'll need and buy them before leaving home. This saves money and gives you incentive to use them while on your trip.

3. Shop Club or Discount Stores. If possible, visit a warehouse club (Costco or Sam's Club) when you first arrive

at your destination to buy foods you can cook at home base. Wine, beer, and alcohol selection and pricing is better at Club or discount stores.

4. Happy Hours. Check out happy hour menus and prices at different spots several times a week. Even if you don't drink alcohol, prices for appetizers and small plates are discounted during happy hour. A couple of appetizers and a happy hour beverage along with a beachside sunset can satisfy your appetite and let you spend less on dinner.

5. Splurge Meals. There's a consumer behavior known "scrimp-splurge" in the marketing world. Shoppers save money by scrimping on items they have little emotional attachment to and splurge on things that bring them joy. For example, a person may scrimp on store brand food staples but splurge on mouth-watering cupcakes for their child's birthday. Apply this concept to your travel food spending. Keep a lid on expenses for most food experiences then splurge when you go enjoy a meal at a nice restaurant. Plan a few "splurge" meals so that you can sample the local flavors and fully experience the destination. If budget is a concern, splurge on lunch instead of dinner. Portions are still plentiful but usually are priced much lower than similar dinner hour options.

6. Farmers' Markets and Picnics. What's better than walking through a local market that's stocked with fresh,

locally grown organic fruits and vegetables? Often, you'll be treated to samples of new foods you've not previously tried. These are great stops along the way to pick up healthy snacks and fixings for a picnic in the park. Let your senses guide you. Stop by the side of the road to pick up some goodies at a fruit stand or spend an hour picking fresh apples or berries in season. Investigate when and where the next farmers' market will be and weave a picnic into your plans.

7. BYOF. You know that BYOB means Bring Your Own Booze. Well, BYOF stands for Bring Your Own Food. With a little planning you can eat healthier and more flavorful fare by bringing fruit, nuts, trail mix, vegetables and hummus, or a turkey sandwich on the first leg of your journey. Put Clif bars in the car for emergency sustenance. Whether you're traveling by airplane, train, automobile, bicycle, ship, skateboard, or your own two feet, BYOF. You'll save money and keep your healthy eating plan on track. Save those extra calories for splurging on a meal or dessert when it really counts.

8. Local Options. Venture away from the freeways and main arteries where all the overpriced chain or franchise eateries are located and find hidden restaurant gems. Ask the locals you meet about their favorite places. Look for food trucks and street vendors — depending on the place where you're visiting. Always try local places that are unique and not "corporate."

Contemplate how you might optimize your food experiences and budget over the next few days or upcoming trip. What action steps will you take this week to begin making a shift?

This is the place to write about your off-the-beaten-path foodie "a-ha!" moments:

## PUBLIC VENUES

Part of the joy of living my life's camino is having the freedom to explore interesting places. No matter where I travel, near or far, exploring new and different local sites and neighborhoods is a major part of my desire for adventure.

I like to get the overview of a new city from a walking tour or a bike tour. I'll wander back later to the sites that pique my curiosity for a more in-depth visit. Bike tours usually offer a low cost option that provides several hours of exercise with a guide who knows the city. I enjoy taking a bike tour as soon as I arrive at a new location if there is any potential for jet lag. It keeps me awake and helps me adjust to the new time zone. Hop-on/hop-off bus tours are a good choice at other times. For one price, you have access to a day or two of paid transportation to the city's major attractions along with plenty of historical and cultural information.

Self-guided walking tours are my favorite. Get a city map from the tourism office and head out on a loop of your own design. This provides flexibility to spend as much time as you like at the locations of greatest interest to you. If you're lucky, you'll find a free guided walking tour. These typically don't require much advance planning and are easily found on sites like TripAdvisor. Walking tours are offered throughout the day and evening, and cover a range of interest areas. Guides appreciate cash tips if they've done a good job but this is always discretionary.

If extensive walking isn't your thing, do a web search before you leave home for things to do at your destination. I use this readily available information to get ideas of unique and interesting sites the most popular tours visit or the media publicizes. Then I chart my own course. Half the fun for me is discovering the possibilities before the trip begins.

I was recently in New York City on a girls' trip. I had part of one day on my own, so I read through information on tours offered and sites of interest near TriBeCa and the Financial District. In addition to visiting the usual tourist stops, I discovered an off-the-beaten-path book store filled with mysterious books, a Japanese knife store with demonstrations and classes on knife sharpening, a 'dream house' experience with magenta lights and pulsating music, a hospital for broken fountain pens, a museum dedicated to neon, and a museum with a vintage poster collection. On my quest to find some of these free public places, I also encountered interesting shops and street food vendors. New York is a special place. There might not be as many of these quirky places in every town but there are little known spots waiting to be discovered everywhere.

Another thing to look for is opportunities for free visits to popular public venues. The national parks in the United States offer free entrance on certain holidays. Many museums offer occasional free evening visiting hours, free days for teachers, and reduced rates for students or seniors. All it takes is a bit of research on the venue's website.

Other interesting locations that are free or have very low entrance fees are places of worship, historic government buildings, markets, and parks. Often there is plenty of historical information on signage throughout the location or available via a free pamphlet. You may hear stories shared by local volunteers that you wouldn't come across on a tour. Not long ago, I was at a church in Spain, attempting to photograph its dome from the floor far below. The local volunteer spoke only a few words of English and I spoke only a few words of Spanish. We somehow managed to converse about the best place for lunch and how to take a picture of the dome from below more easily using "selfie" mode. Discoveries abound when you're traversing locations outside the confines of a large tour group.

Here's a great tip: Inquire at your hotel about free experiences and/or activities they may offer. It's a great way to connect with others vacationing in the area as well as try your hand at a few unique activities. In Fiji, the place I stayed offered island tours, a basket weaving experience, snorkel use, and a kava drinking ceremony — all for free. In Hawaii, I found lei making classes, an introductory scuba lesson at the pool, opportunities to paint and decorate souvenir coconuts, and movie nights, including popcorn — all for free. Near home, I learned about a free tequila tasting event with mariachi band, a free kaleidoscope convention, and a free chef-led kitchen tour at an upscale restaurant. I discovered all of these stops along the way because I was curious and talked to locals.

Contemplate a few types of interesting local experiences you might enjoy and research them. What action steps will you take this week to begin making a shift?

What "a-ha!"s have you discovered in public venues, and for free?

## GET AFTER IT

Giving back through volunteerism is also a type of stop along the way. Volunteerism is something that can be done every day, every week, month, or even once a year. When you volunteer, you give of yourself, and your time to increase the amount of wellbeing and joy that exists in the world.

Both of my sons were active in high school, sampling many of the social, athletic, academic and leadership opportunities that came their way. Team sports were always a high priority. For both the exercise and its life lessons, these teachable moments began when the kids were very young. Victory, defeat, sportsmanship, fairness, bad calls, compassion, collaboration, leadership, discipline, preparedness, respect, and camaraderie are just a few of those lessons. My youngest son chose to play football in high school. He learned the game under the guidance of a number of great coaches including Scot Bemis. One of Scot's mantras was "Get After It" — as in, 'let's put our heart and soul into everything we do on and off the field.'

During my son's sophomore year football season, his coach was diagnosed with metastasized lung cancer. The boys rallied and played hard for a man for whom they had the greatest respect. Scot died a few months later at age 45. This was the first time most of the boys had dealt with death and it was a difficult lesson. In Scot's honor, a founding group of dedicated parents began a flag football fundraiser that's held Thanksgiving morning every year. It's named the Bemis Bowl after Scot and it's played on his namesake Bemis field at the high school. Funds raised go to the Bemis foundation to support student scholarships. He was, and still is, an inspiration to us all.

This latest chilly Thanksgiving morning, 100+ volunteers arrived at the field at 6 am for the 8th annual Bemis bowl. Over 1000 parents, alumni, and current students spent the first half of their Thanksgiving Day remembering a man that some had played for and years later others knew only as a legend.

This stop along the way reminds me of the importance of giving of my time. We each get 24 hours in a day. When you choose to spend some of this precious time in the service of others, a ripple effect of joy and inspiration is created. I strive to become a joy magnifier. The best way to feel joy in your life is by enhancing joy in the lives of others.

When you fully embrace and live your life's camino, you too have the potential to create a ripple effect on the lives of others. I think of Scot's mantra "Get After It" and I'm reminded to "get after" my own life, to dream big, and take small steps every day. To stop waiting for permission or letting other people's agenda dictate where I'm going or how I'm spending my time.

Contemplate how you might use your skills in service of the community. What action steps will you take this week to begin making a shift?

Have you ever experienced an "a-ha!" related to time you spent as a volunteer?

## HOLIDAY TRADITIONS

Along your life's camino each place you pause, however briefly, is a stop on your journey. Holiday traditions create memories. Traditions also simplify life because each time the experience is repeated it makes a new "groove" on the track and requires less effort to bring the enjoyment to life. Think about how your traditions take on positive energy of their own that draws you back into them year after year.

Holidays can be stressful times. Memories of the death of beloved family members and pets can make you feel sad during the holidays when you miss their participation in the traditions. Perhaps your family has experienced divorce, and the old traditions have given way to new ones. For others, just getting along with family members during the holiday can be a challenge. There are ways to leave some of the stresses behind and let holiday traditions elevate your spirit.

Traditions are a big part of who I am. It all began when I was 6 or 7 years old. Following an afternoon Christmas Mass, we'd rush home to a fondue meal — appetizer-sized portions fried in hot oil. Pizza rolls, onion rings, tater tots, chicken, and beef created a smorgasbord of options. During my high school years, a cheese fondue was added. Nearly 50 years later, I continue this tradition with my adult children, their significant others, my brother and his family, and my parents. We're all fond of fondue as a Christmas tradition!

Another annual tradition I greatly enjoy is a neighborhood ornament exchange party. Two good friends have co-hosted this event for more than 15 years. The date is always set for a Thursday in early December. It's a fun evening exchanging holiday ornaments in an anonymous way. Friends of all faith traditions participate. It's not about the ornament or the Christmas holiday. It's about friends sharing a joy-filled evening together.

Traditions bring joy. While there's no price on joy, traditions don't need to be cost prohibitive. Living my life's camino is about making time with family and friends a priority. In my mind there's no better way to reinforce that than through shared traditions.

If your family hasn't established many traditions, imagine a few memorable experiences from your youth and start a new tradition. Blend traditions from yours and your significant other's family to give them a new twist. These stops along the road are among the most worth it.

Contemplate whether expanding the role of traditions is important for your life's camino. What action steps will you take this week to begin making a shift?

Noticing the "a-ha!" moments about holiday and other traditions is what makes them valuable. What are some of yours?

## HEART GIFTS

The tradition of gift giving is a focus at certain holidays. It's true that magic happens when you give gifts from the heart at any time of the year. That's why all those handmade cards and glued macaroni art projects from your child's elementary school years can bring a tear to your eye. The key to staying in heart-gift mode is setting a lower than average dollar amount for gift giving. The actual amount is unimportant as long as it pushes you to be creative in order to make the gift special. Heart gifts are cherished because they are personal, unique, and thoughtful.

One of our family's heart gift traditions began when my sons were young children. It's a re-interpretation of the Advent calendar we call "25 Days Of Christmas." Advent calendars have 25 small doors, one for each December day leading to Christmas. The doors have a treat or a piece of chocolate behind them. In late November each year, a "25 Days Of Christmas" participant receives a box containing 25 small, individually wrapped gifts. Each day they randomly choose a gift to open. This activity is especially fun now that my sons are adults and live away from home. They enjoy a daily moment that brings the spirit of Christmas to them. The total cost of the box of 25 gifts is capped at $100. With a few "big ticket" $10 gift cards included, the average price of each remaining gift is around $3. It's not about the gifts, but rather the element of surprise and joy they feel opening a colorfully wrapped package created especially for them.

Another holiday gifting concept I've enjoyed also involves inexpensive, creatively inspired items. The giver puts together a collection of small gifts that recap the recipient's most important activities or milestones that year. Perhaps it's an ornament that represents a location they've visited, a memento from an event, or a coloring book that represents a new hobby. As each gift is opened, the person has to figure out how it connects with their journey. A different spin on this concept is to assemble a collection of items important for the next year's journey, such as spare shoelaces for the hiking shoes to be used on the next trip, a candle to light the way, a jar of after dinner mints for a party the recipient will be hosting. These forward-thinking gifts are extra special.

Make time for the people you care about. Do something special when you create a gift for them. It will create magical memories for them and do even more for you.

Contemplate how you might dial up your creativity and design a heart-gift for an upcoming birthday or holiday. What action steps will you take this week to begin making a shift?

Write two "a-ha!"s — one about making, and one about giving gifts:

# RECEIVING

Are you practiced in the art of receiving? It seems odd, but receiving is actually much harder than giving. Givers look for ways to make people smile by sharing gifts. Givers need people around them who know how to receive in order for them fully feel the joy of giving.

I learned to hone my receiving skills while on vacation with a close-knit group of long time girlfriends at a place I love to visit: Miraval Resort in Tucson, Arizona. It has flavorful healthy meals, a great selection of activities, seminars, speakers, spa treatments, and experiences that allow its visitors to renew, recharge, and grow.

One of my favorite presenters at Miraval is Tejpal. (www.Tejpal-Inspires.com) She's an intuitive, spiritually grounded person traveling a fascinating life camino with interesting stops as a corporate leadership development expert, author, healer, and life coach. Check out her books on Amazon. My favorite is *Manifest Moment to Moment: 8 Principles to Create the Life You Truly Desire*. Listening to her speak always opens my mind to new ways of thinking. In one session I attended, she spoke about the importance of receiving.

My takeaway from her message was that with giving one remains in control. Humans like control because it maintains a comfort zone and reduces risk of unexpected emotions or embarrassment. When you learn to receive, you open yourself up to what "is." You stop trying to control and you allow, you go with the flow, and can just be. Receiving is a state of being present. When you truly receive, you open your heart to what the giver is offering, and you make an emotional connection with them.

I learned a great deal about how to improve my receiving skills through an exercise Tejpal recommended. I'll share it with you.

Get a journal. Each day for the next six weeks set aside a short amount of time to sit in quiet and ask the question, "What did I receive today?" Jot down whatever comes to mind. It's easy for your mind to wander and to think you must be finished after a week. Keep going. It's different from a gratitude journal, although both practices ultimately help fuel one's "joy-meter."

This exercise challenged me to pay attention to what I was receiving. My lists started out with things like, "I received a compliment about my hair." As days went by I started noticing more subtle and meaningful insights. "I received the gift of a glorious Arizona sunrise." Or, "I received a sweet kiss from my dog that made me smile."

Honing my receiving skills has made me a better giver. I improved my ability to focus on what the person I was giving to most needed to receive. I asked for help, which gave others an opportunity to practice giving. I was clear about saying what I needed so people who wanted to give to me could really deliver. As I focused on receiving, I became more present. This made me more appreciative of the giving happening all around me. A giving — receiving cycle emerged that created positive ripples through my friends and family.

Contemplate how you might practice receiving authentically. Commit to completing the receiving exercise described earlier. What action steps will you take this week to begin making a shift?

Write an "a-ha!" about receiving:

# THE LAST WORD

Now you know how I transformed my life's camino. Interestingly, the Spanish word "camino" means "path" and as a conjugation of the verb caminar also means "I walk". It took a few years, and a lot of baby steps walking my path to arrive at this point. I'm nowhere near done! As I reflect on this stage of the journey, I can see the 180-degree transformation I've made from living life on other people's terms to living my dream life on my terms. My hope is that some of these ideas will inspire you to take action in your life, to step it up, to embrace and evolve your life's camino.

Look back through the sections of the book, the notes you made, and the actions you took. If you read all the way through the first time, consider going back, re-reading, and taking action on one of the sections each week over the course of a year. Think about which ideas will deliver the most helpful changes for you and take more small steps in those areas. Lasting changes were never accomplished in a day or even a month. It's a marathon not a sprint.

Most people do a lot more talking than taking action. Will you let yourself fall into this trap? Reimagining and repositioning your life's camino requires only small amounts of time and money. Your relationship status is irrelevant. You don't need to be single, married, or in any specific life stage to make your dream life happen. Please remember my mistakes, where I spent a lot of time in my head thinking, planning, worrying, and telling myself things like, "not now, later" or "I'm not ready." Don't waste time on this. Stop waiting for the perfect time. You know everything you need to know at this very moment to get started. You'll learn along the way what you need to know for later steps that you can't possibly imagine now.

Transforming my life's camino came down to three things: 1) letting go of my excuses (fear), 2) mustering up the courage to venture to places that I felt were uncomfortable, and 3) taking action consistently in the form of small steps in the general direction of my hopes and dreams. In some ways, I wish I knew then what I know now. I didn't need to have it all figured out. I just needed to get started.

There's a quote I remember from years ago. It's always spoken to me and sums up the spirit of this camino-inspired book perfectly. It gets to the heart of the opportunity in front of us — to embrace and joyfully reimagine the path of our life's camino.

*Do not go where the path may lead. Go instead where there is no path and leave a trail.*

~ *Ralph Waldo Emerson*

# ABOUT THE AUTHOR

Liz Harvey is an author, public speaker, and former business executive in the consumer packaged goods industry. With two business partners she owns Quintessent Marketing, a boutique consulting firm that helps companies transform and grow their business interests.

Most often, Liz can be found on the road, exploring off-the-grid destinations near and far. She has fully embraced her inner "travelista" and enjoys meeting people across the globe to share stories of finding joy and living life on one's own terms.

An official devotee of life camino-ing, she's reimagined her life path and inspires others with her stories and down-to-earth, easy-to-implement, practical steps to life transformation amidst the chaos of everyday life.

Liz has two adult sons and calls Scottsdale, Arizona home.

Follow Liz on Instagram and Facebook at **TravelistaLiz** or her on blog **TravelistaLiz.com**

## LIZ HARVEY'S
# LETTER TO READERS

Camino Mates,

I'm delighted to officially welcome you to the tribe. I'm looking forward to hearing your stories and sharing life lessons as we traverse unique life caminos and explore the amazing world at our toes and fingertips.

I'd love to stay connected and if you'd like that too, social media is definitely our best option. At our blog (www.travelistaliz.com) you'll find updates and stories from the community as well as links to resources mentioned in the book. We'd love to hear your life camino story and what main lesson or inspiration came to you from reading the book. Include a photo if you like. These stories will be compiled and shared at a future date.

Finally, would you please help us spread the Camino message by leaving a review on Amazon?

Buen Camino!

*Travelista Liz*

Made in the USA
Columbia, SC
03 June 2019